PASSING IT ON

bright sky press
HOUSTON, TEXAS

2365 Rice Boulevard, Suite 202,
Houston, Texas 77005

10 9 8 7 6 5 4 3 2

Library of Congress Cataloging-in-Publication Data
Baker, Susan G., 1938-
Passing it on : an autobiography with spirit / Susan G. Baker.
p. cm.
ISBN 978-1-933979-84-7 (hardcover)
1. Baker, Susan G., 1938- 2. Christian biography.
3. Politician's spouses—United States—Biography. 4. Baker, James Addison, 1930- I. Title.

BR1725.B26A3 2010
277.3'082092—dc22   2010008588
[B]

I gratefully acknowledge the authors, publishers and photographers whose
words and images I have used in this book, including these:

Holy Bible, New International Version. "Scripture taken from the New King James Version.
Copyright © 1982 by Thomas Nelson, Inc. Used by permission. All rights reserved."

Ruth Meyers with Warren Meyers, 31 Days of Praise: Enjoying God Anew, Mutnomah Publishers, Inc. (2002)

Cover photo © Wallace W. McNamee/Corbis
The Cattleman magazine, page 91; Official White House Photographs, pages 95, 97, 99, 104, 105, 107; Mary Garrett, page 93;
Kaye Marvins Photography, page 96; *Time Magazine* with photos by Dennis Brack, Paul Natkin,
Judas Priest-Terry Sesvold/PixIntl, Twisted Sister-Rick Gould/PixIntl, page 98; The State Department, pages 100, 101;
Caron S. Jackson, page 103; Paul Marchand, page 106; Jeff Lamppert Photography, page 108;
Printed in Canada.

PASSING IT ON

AN AUTOBIOGRAPHY WITH SPIRIT

SUSAN G. BAKER

b bright sky press
HOUSTON, TEXAS

With love to my family—
past, present, and to come

Prologue

Passing the baton to the next generation is one of the most important assignments of a parent and grandparent, yet today we often live far removed from our children and grandchildren. Even when they dwell nearby, busy schedules often torpedo our hopes for regular family visits. What is lost, besides the pleasure of each other's company, are the stories that are not told, the values that are not passed along, and the sense of connectedness and family that are not strengthened by the age-old means—spending time together.

This book is intended to help close that separation, and to pass the baton through the printed word. It is about living life as a daughter, wife, mother, grandmother, friend, and citizen, and about the lessons I have learned along the way. It is written with love for my family, with the prayer that it may help lighten their load and cheer their days.

I also write this book to thank friends outside my family for all they have given me over the years, and to share my experiences with other readers who may pick it up and find words of encouragement. This is not a book on history or theology, though I have lived through a lot of history and I love God. I'm just trying to tell my story.

The title comes from a special experience I had with a dear neighbor, Neva Pickens. Neva and her husband, Pick, lived across the street when I was expecting Elizabeth, my first child, and they were a wonderful help and comfort to me. They had three great kids, and for six years their daughters, Penny and Vonnie, were our family babysitters. I couldn't have survived without their help or without the sage advice and support Neva gave me during a difficult time in my first marriage.

When my family moved away from the neighborhood, I was distraught at leaving my special friend. I remember saying to her, "Neva, how can I ever repay you for all you have done for us?" She smiled her wonderful smile and said, "Just pass it on, darlin'."

It took me a while to understand the significance of these words. In this culture we seem loath to accept a gift without feeling obligated to repay in kind. For a long while, I felt guilty that there was no tangible way to express my real gratitude to Neva. Gradually, however, I learned the lesson of "passing it on" to others, and that is what this little book is all about.

Acknowledgments

I am forever grateful to all the people who have influenced my life, especially my beloved family and special friends. Also my many wonderful teachers—at school, in church and Bible study, and through books, tapes, and commentaries. For this book project I am particularly grateful to Jeanie Miley, whose staunch encouragement gave me the courage to actually begin, and once begun, to share my stories with a wider audience. My desire to accomplish this has been fulfilled in large measure due to her help and moral support. As important as Jeanie's support has been, there would not be a book without Darrell Hancock's excellent editing and research. I am indebted to both of these special and gifted people for helping make this book a reality.

I'm so thankful for my wonderful husband and my amazing daughters Elizabeth and Mary Bonner who contributed invaluable insights and affirmation during this process. To my sister and best friend Klinka Lollar, dear pal Sara McIntosh, and mentor, the Reverend John K. Graham, M.D., go bountiful thanks for their willingness to read my manuscript and offer helpful ideas and suggestions. A heartfelt thank you also goes to the team at Bright Sky Press—to Rue Judd for her warm friendship and belief in my project, to Lucy Chambers and Cristina Adams for their fine editing skills, and to Ellen Cregan for the book design. They turned a daunting task into a fun endeavor for me.

Most of all I am beholden to my parents, who passed along the strong values and abiding love of God that have lighted every step of my path. Mountains of gratitude and affection go to Juanita Young Navy, who played a major supporting role in many of the events described in this book, and who retired in 2009 after thirty-five years of dedicated service to our family. To my eight wonderful children—Elizabeth, Bo, Will, Jamie, Stuart, John, Doug, and Mary Bonner—you are my hopes fulfilled and prayers answered. I thank God for all the things you've taught me along the way! And, of course, I am forever indebted to the love of my life, Jimmy Baker, who has loved me, supported me, and encouraged and enabled me to do things I might otherwise never have dreamed of doing. Thank you, darling, for a wild and wonderful ride!

TABLE OF CONTENTS

Chapter One

WAHOO—WE ARE STILL STANDING!
ೕᴥ

FOR THE FIRST TWENTY YEARS OF OUR MARRIED LIFE JIM BAKER AND I DIDN'T TAKE OUR CHILDREN ON MANY REAL VACATIONS. FOR ALMOST FIFTEEN OF THOSE YEARS, WE LIVED ON A GOVERNMENT SCHEDULE (AND SALARY!), AND THERE JUST NEVER SEEMED TO BE ENOUGH TIME OR RESOURCES. OUR PROMISE TO EACH OTHER AFTER WE RETIRED FROM GOVERNMENT SERVICE IN JANUARY 1993 WAS THAT WE WOULD MAKE UP FOR LOST TIME. OUR TRIP TO OLYMPIC VALLEY IN 2007, NESTLED IN THE SIERRA NEVADA RANGE OF CALIFORNIA, WAS ANOTHER INSTALLMENT ON THAT PROMISE.

It was a wonderful happening when thirty-five members of our immediate family gathered at a resort near Lake Tahoe in August of 2007. We ranged in age from two to seventy-seven years, and miracle of miracles, there wasn't one cross word during our almost five days together!

Jim and I had joined forces exactly thirty-four years earlier. He had four boys, and I had a daughter and two sons. (Four years later we would add another daughter.) From the beginning, it was a combustible household. Friends were incredulous when we married, and some thought we were crazy.

Now, all these years later, we were together in California celebrating the fact that we had survived as an eclectic, but loving, family. Despite all the complications, despite the ups and downs, despite the odds, despite everything, we were standing strong.

The golfing, hiking, and rafting we did were great, but the best times were just sitting around the pool and talking, talking, talking.

No meetings. No carpools. No trips to the grocery. Just three generations of family enjoying each other.

Late Sunday afternoon we had a family prayer service. We thanked God for our many blessings, remembered dear ones lost, and prayed for our family and the nation. There was a very powerful moment as our eighteen-year-old grandson asked if he could give his own prayer. This kid had had a tough time growing up, especially because his mother had not lived with him and his sister since he was six. He had dropped out of school for a while but had recently chosen to deal with his problems, and we were thrilled that he was there with us.

There wasn't a dry eye on that balcony as he said this prayer:

Dearest Almighty Creator,
I take this time to thank You for the blessings
You have granted me throughout my life.
I thank You for Blood, Body, and Spirit.
For Blood,
My family who guides me.
For Body,
My friends, who—like family—support me in my trials.
And for Spirit.
Every moment in my life, I am alive—good and bad,
Which I am rewarded with for the actions I have made.
These are the blessings only You can provide:
Blood,
Body,
And Spirit.
Amen

The Chief—that's what the grandchildren call Jim—had a big lump in his throat as he told this young man how proud we all were of him. Then Jim gave a short, powerful talk about letting God be God, not trying to play God ourselves.

Speaking especially to the grandchildren, Jim said that early on he thought he had to do it all by himself. He should be independent, strong, he thought, not needing or depending on others. Then he found out he was wrong. In fact, he did need God. And he needed other people in his life—most of all, his family.

That touching prayer service wasn't our only blessing that Sunday.

Earlier in the day, Jim and I had visited our old friends, Carolyn and Mike Deaver. They had a summer home about an hour away at Fallen Leaf Lake and had invited us to attend the christening service for two grandchildren at nearby St. Francis of the Mountains Episcopal Church.

After the service in the quaint log-cabin church, we shared a delicious lunch on the Deavers' deck overlooking the lake. As we ate, we reminisced about our time together in the Reagan administration. After the 1980 election, Mike and Stu Spencer had lobbied Ronald Reagan to hire Jim as White House chief of staff. Mike and Jim had then been part of the famous "troika" (along with Ed Meese) that served President Reagan during his first term. On this bright sunny afternoon we told stories, some of which I had never heard before, and the good memories and laughter cheered us.

It was a poignant time, as Mike was battling pancreatic cancer, and we all knew that the battle was almost over. Within several weeks he would die and Jim would speak at his memorial service. On this day, however—sitting on the deck between a deep blue sky and the rippling water, surrounded by family and friends—Mike reflected on life. "It doesn't get any better than this," he said.

On the drive back to rejoin our family, memories of the Reagan years flooded my mind. What unexpected and fascinating times Jim and I had lived.

* * *

The weather was cool and overcast as dawn broke over our nation's capital on January 20, 1981. Shortly before noon, Jim and I were ushered to our seats on the inaugural platform over the steps on the west front of the Capitol.

My heart was pounding. I was amazed that I, a country girl from Brazoria County, Texas, was there, sitting among the leaders of our nation—Supreme Court justices, senators, House leaders and soon-to-be cabinet officers!

The Capitol Building and the platform were hung with gigantic red, white, and blue banners. At the base of the white-walled platform, the U.S. Marine Band played patriotic music and at least one hymn, "God of our Fathers." Rising in front of the platform was a tower for reporters and television cameras. Thousands upon thousands of spectators filled the Capitol grounds and spilled onto the adjoining National Mall. Our children were seated just below the podium, but the high angle blocked them from our view. In the distance were the Washington Monument and, barely visible over the horizon, the Lincoln Memorial.

"Can you believe this?" I whispered to Jim. "Pinch me so I'll know I'm not dreaming!"

At the appointed hour, the president-elect placed his left hand on his mother's old Bible, raised his right hand, and recited the solemn and timeless presidential oath: "I, Ronald Wilson Reagan, do solemnly swear…so help me God."

He then kissed Nancy, resplendent in red, and stepped to the microphone, smiling broadly as wave upon wave of cheers rose from the crowd. When it finally grew quiet, he pledged a new beginning for America, with a revitalized economy and a stronger national defense.

Just as the speech ended, the bright January sun cut through the gray clouds like a celestial spotlight, illuminating and warming the brilliant white Capitol Building, the enthusiastic crowd, and—symbolically at least—our nation's very heart and soul. And at almost that exact moment, we would soon learn, two airplanes had lifted off in Iran, freeing fifty-two American hostages after 444 agonizing days in captivity.

That day in 1981 marked a rebirth of our great nation's spirit of hope and optimism. What a wonderful privilege it was to have been there. The experience was a profound one for me, almost magical.

As we stood together on the inaugural platform that day, Jim and I had been husband and wife for seven and one-half years. The journey from our simple—and very private—marriage ceremony in Houston, Texas to this magnificent public celebration in Washington, D.C., had been full of love, but it had also been arduous and, at times, painful.

* * *

When we married in August of 1973, I expected that I would have a relatively normal life as a big-firm lawyer's wife in Texas. Certainly there would be bumps in the road as we merged two sets of children—his four, my three—into one big, happy family. But others had done it and so could we.

Little did I know.

Two years into our marriage, my expectations took a detour. My husband, the Houston lawyer, was invited to serve as under secretary of commerce for President Gerald Ford. Suddenly I was looking for a place to live in Washington, and I was also trying to find someone to stay in our Houston house with a son who was finishing his senior year of high school.

And that was just the beginning. In the fall of 1976, about a year after we moved to Washington, Jim took charge of President Ford's campaign; our bonus baby, Mary Bonner, was born the following year. The next few years kept him busy, as he ran for attorney general of Texas and then served for two years as chairman of George H. W. Bush's campaign for the Republican presidential nomination. But the big surprise came in August 1980, when Ronald Reagan, then GOP candidate for president, asked Jim to join his campaign team.

An even bigger surprise came immediately after the November election: President-elect Reagan asked my husband to serve as his White House chief of staff. I should have been happy, but I was devastated.

For one thing, we had five precious teens still at home, many of them doing things they shouldn't have been doing, and all needing more time with their dad, not less. My exhausted body and spirit rebelled against having to dismantle our Houston house, find another place to live, set up housekeeping again, and begin a whole new life, while coping with one three-year-old and a handful of rebellious adolescents. The idea of having to attend endless official Washington social events and juggle these family concerns—and doing it all in a fishbowl—was more than I wanted to handle. True, this was an amazing honor and opportunity for Jim, but our family was struggling and fragmented.

All I really wanted to do was take everyone home to Houston and collapse.

Jim told Ronald Reagan how upset I was, and why. White House chief of staff is one of the most demanding jobs in government. Jim would be so thoroughly consumed by the job that I knew we would never see him. He would drag home at night after we were all in bed, then melt away once again before the sun rose.

A few days later, Ronald Reagan put his arm around me and assured me that I had nothing to worry about. "Your husband is not going to work fourteen hours a day in my White House. I don't believe in that," he said. "I believe in my people spending time with their families. Jim will be home at six o'clock every evening."

The president-to-be was sincere in his promise. Every time he saw me in the first year, he would ask if Jim was getting home early enough. I would force myself to smile when I replied, "Not yet, Mr. President." Of course I knew in my heart that Jim's desire to do the best possible job would consume all the hours of his days.

In November 1980, I was just *tired;* I exhausted myself even further by telling God, again and again, that I just didn't approve of His plan for our lives. Of course Jim hit the ground running to prepare for the new Reagan administration, but it took weeks before I reluctantly relinquished my dream of a "regular life." Choosing to trust that God's grace would be enough for whatever lay ahead was a struggle, but I knew that was what I had to do.

The next twelve years, beginning with President Reagan's first inauguration and ending with President Clinton's swearing in, were a fabulous, life-changing adventure that I will always treasure, in spite of the difficulties. Jim was *meant* for politics and public service, and I was *meant* to serve alongside him as his wife, as mother to our children and—although I did not know it at the time— as a citizen-volunteer on several very important issues that touched my heart.

My decision to surrender to the sufficiency of God's grace changed my life and the life of our family. It also meant that I had the honor of playing a part in the life of our nation and the world through Jim's years of dedicated public service.

Chapter Two

CHOCOLATE PIE FOR BREAKFAST
ৰ৸৶

MEMORIES FROM MY CHILDHOOD STILL BRING ME PLEASURE: SWINGING FROM GRAPEVINES, FINDING THE FIRST VIOLETS PEEKING FROM UNDER THE LEAVES IN THE SPRING, RUNNING THROUGH THE WOODS DODGING YELLOW-AND-BLACK SPIDERS' WEBS, EATING LUNCH ON THE FRONT PORCH TO THE CRICKETS' SERENADE, SNEAKING BEHIND THE SMOKEHOUSE TO PUFF ON STRAWS FILLED WITH COFFEE, PICKING DEWBERRIES, SHOOTING SNAKES IN THE RICE CANALS, SLIDING ON THE ICE IN MY RUBBER BOOTS, ATTENDING CATTLE SHOWS, SHARING DELICIOUS DAYLONG HOLIDAY LUNCHES WITH RELATIVES. BUT MY MOST FAVORITE WAS RIDING IN THE PICKUP WITH PAPPY—THAT'S WHAT WE GARRETT CHILDREN CALLED OUR FATHER—AS HE TALKED TO ME ABOUT CROPS AND CATTLE. I EVEN FELT THAT WAY AFTER IT DAWNED ON ME THAT HIS MAIN PURPOSE IN INVITING ME ALONG WAS TO HAVE ME TO OPEN AND CLOSE ALL THE GATES!

My dad's full name was John Travis Garrett, but he went by Jack. In 1936 he bought land near Danbury, Texas, and started growing rice and raising cattle. From the time he was a boy he had said that he would marry a beautiful lady and live on a ranch. When he wed Mary Blackshear Farish, a young widow whose husband, Jeff D. Farish, had died in a plane crash, his boast became a reality. Despite the concerns of her friends, my mother loved moving to the country, and she cherished raising her family in the peaceful atmosphere of Brazoria County. All four children had chores, but Pappy was a lot more demanding of the boys than of my sister and me. Five-thirty a.m. reveille was mandatory for the boys, but we girls would often sleep in until 6:30. At harvest time, the young Garretts rode the trucks and combines. We also helped work the cattle. Hired ranch hands did most of the work, of course, but we were expected to participate.

The term *hired hands* doesn't do justice in describing the relationships we children had with the very special people who were around us as we grew up. There were many, but the three that had the greatest impact were African Americans, Willie and Irvin (called Son) Cooper and Wil Shook. Wil, who was a wise soul about ranch life, and life in general, came to work on the land when Pappy purchased it. His patience in showing us the ropes had a profound effect, especially on my brothers. Willie and Son, who had no children at that time, lived behind our house and loved us like we were their own. This included chasing us down the road with a hairbrush when we were naughty! They were with us for more than fifty years, and Son was the first person to be buried in our family cemetery.

The worst job the Garrett children ever had to do was pick cotton. We didn't grow it ourselves, but our father would farm us out to neighbors who were in a bind. In the era before mechanical harvesters, we would trudge up and down the rows, hour after hour, dragging our heavy sacks and filling them with the cotton we pulled from the sharp dry husks. We earned 50¢ for every hundred pounds we lugged back to the wagon, which was big money at the time. But this was small compensation for our weary bodies and sore fingers. Fortunately we didn't have to do it often, but this gave us a real appreciation for hard, backbreaking work—and for those who did it.

My father raised Brahman cattle—large, silver-gray animals with a hump on their shoulders, long, floppy ears, and a high tolerance for Texas heat, mosquitoes, and disease. Each year, Pappy would give each kid a calf to raise. Brahmans have a shy disposition and are easily startled, so the trick was to gentle them with kindness. The radio in the show barn was always tuned in to the country-and-western station; a little Roy Acuff or Eddie Arnold soothed the animals and helped us forget we would rather be doing something else.

The payoff came during the cattle shows, including the wonderful State Fair of Texas in Dallas each October. We would groom our heifers and bulls, then lead them out into the ring to be graded by the judges. The goal was to come home with a ribbon. We did it for fun, but there was a serious purpose, too. Pappy sold breeding stock, and show-ring victories were good for his business.

Some of my happiest memories are of the trips to the stock shows. All rules were off. Pappy never made us take baths, and we could order anything we wanted for our meals, even chocolate pie for breakfast!

Our family ranch was five miles north of Danbury, a small farming community on the Texas coastal plains. The population in the forties and fifties was less than 500. The Missouri-Pacific Railroad ran straight through the middle of our town, right past the large rice dryers that Pappy built in 1943 with the help of German prisoners of war. (Pappy loved to fly and wanted to join the Army Air Corps in World War ll, but he was told by the draft board that it was more important to the war effort for him to stay home and produce rice and beef.)

The common mode of transportation in Danbury was a pickup truck, and flour-sack dresses and outhouses were not unusual. We kids wore blue jeans with boots in the cool weather and tennis shoes or bare feet in the spring, summer, and fall. Glitz and glamour were not part of our vocabulary.

I was the firstborn, followed twenty-one months later by my rambunctious, black-eyed sister Klinka. Her real name was Carolyn, but my baby talk mispronunciation of it suited her so well that she has made it her legal name as an adult. The first son, John Travis Garrett, Jr, known as Jacko, has our father's strength, but his personality is as gentle as Pappy's was rough. Robert King Garrett (Bob) was the baby, but he gave as good as he got, and he is the most independent of us all. We were a high-spirited bunch with a lot of freedom, but our strong and loving parents also expected us to toe the line. And we generally did.

But we also made time for fun. We were members of the Texas Corinthian Yacht Club on Galveston Bay. Before the days of air conditioning, we would go to the bay to escape the heat for several weeks at a time. Pappy would fly down in his small plane at the end of the day, landing on a grass strip across the road. There we fished, swam, and learned to sail. We really enjoyed having summertime friends within walking distance, because at the ranch we had to travel miles to find a playmate. Some of our TCYC friends are still among our closest pals today.

As I have mentioned, we called our father Pappy, but our friends and neighbors had a different name for him—Whispering Jack. That was a joke, because his voice was like an amplified *foghorn*. He had a generous and caring heart, but his word was loud and it was law. Later in life he grew a beard, he always chewed tobacco, and if you crossed him you were in trouble. Several pipeline companies found this out when they strayed off of their easements one too many times and found their tires shot flat!

My father was a great businessman—a risk-taker and innovator in his farming and ranching. He also followed the best practices in soil and water conservation at a time when the word *environmentalist* hadn't yet been coined.

Over the years, Pappy also helped raise a lot of other people's children. He could always be counted on to provide a bed, three meals a day, leather gloves, and posthole diggers to teenagers who needed attitude adjustments. A few weeks on a working Texas ranch helped many city youngsters learn what we country cousins already knew—the value of discipline and hard work, and the satisfaction of a job well done at the end of the day.

Pappy's strong, demanding personality was beautifully balanced by our mother, a loving nurturer of the first order. She was as beautiful on the inside as she was on the outside, and her heart was as strong as her manner was quiet and gentle. Mary Garrett saw the best in people and refused to be shocked at anything. Her deep faith gave her wisdom, and her love of God translated into a way of life that influenced countless people, within and outside our family circle.

Mom's passion was to put her faith into action by helping others. In 1958, she started a clothing center for the needy at the old Brazoria County Courthouse in Angleton, about ten miles away. She was also a charter member, and later chairman, of the county child welfare unit. She volunteered at the county family service center, the local welfare planning council, the American Red Cross, the Brazoria County Historical Museum, and what is today called

Angleton Danbury Medical Center.

Our parents were dedicated Republicans when that was almost a hanging offense in Texas, and they campaigned hard for local, state, and national GOP candidates. They attended local and state party conventions and contributed financially to candidates and the party. At one time, Mom even served on the executive committee that ran the Texas party. In the mid-1960s, Pappy ran for the statewide office of commissioner of agriculture, not because he expected to win—Democrats controlled Texas for more than a century after the end of Reconstruction in 1876—but to help build a fledgling Republican Party. His campaign budget was less than $5,000, which he amplified with his loud voice, strong personality, and unwavering principles. Whispering Jack didn't win but he did better than expected, and we were very proud of him for being willing to throw his hat into the ring.

What was it like to grow up with such strong, active parents? Well, for one thing, whining from the sidelines was absolutely unacceptable. Mom and Pappy agreed on that point and modeled it into the way they lived. If there was a problem, whether in the family, the business, or the community, we all had a responsibility to help solve it. Mom's active volunteer work, for instance, inspired all four children to try to follow her example. And our parents' political activism inspired Klinka and me to be politically active throughout our lives. My early experience in what was then a small and unpopular party also gave me a good, thick hide.

Faith also played a major role in our community and in our family. Most everybody in Danbury went to either the Catholic or the Baptist church. For us, it seemed impossible to be in the farming business, totally dependent on the weather and faraway markets, and not have some kind of faith.

In the Garrett household, missing Sunday mass was not an option, and saying the blessing and our prayers were everyday activities. So, too, was an awareness that life is a gift to be lived gratefully and fully.

My first memory of church is of a mass in Pappy's warehouse in Danbury. The church—St. Anthony's—had burned down, and Pappy loaned the use of the storage space in his rice dryer until a new church could be built.

I also remember having a fit trying to keep a hat on Klinka's head during mass on many Sundays. She was two and I was four…a bossy big sister from the beginning.

The theology was very old-school in those days, very letter of the law. Mom was an Episcopalian and didn't always go to mass with us. I was horrified to learn in catechism class that she wouldn't go to heaven because she wasn't a Catholic. It was even more terrifying to learn from my best friend in first grade, a Baptist, that I couldn't go to heaven because I *was* a Catholic!

Today, thank goodness, Danbury is a very ecumenical town, with the Catholics, Baptists, and Quakers praying together and collaborating on many projects. My Mom and my brother, Jacko, both played roles in this development. Mom converted to Catholicism in the mid-1950s, and one of her last requests was to have representatives from each church in Danbury present at the altar when the priest performed her funeral mass. It was a beautiful moment; even the most conservative Protestant and Catholic attendees were touched by this spirit of unity in our community.

Klinka and I left Danbury when we were in the eighth and ninth grades to go to boarding school. Our parents believed that our education was one thing people couldn't take away from us, so it was important to get a good one. At that time, the school system in Danbury was subpar by their standards. Klinka and I both wanted to try boarding school, but it was still a scary prospect.

After a year at Marymount in Virginia, I came home to join Klinka at St. Mary's Academy on a gorgeous ten-acre site north of downtown Austin. Two years later, our parents moved us to Houston, where we attended the Kinkaid School. Klinka and I lived in an apartment on Steele Street with Ouida Gray, an art teacher from St. Thomas University. We faced two major problems: cooking our own meals and making our guy friends understand that there would be no beer parties. By the map, Mom and Pappy were thirty-five miles away, but the Garrett sisters were acutely aware of the trust they had placed in us, and we weren't about to disappoint them.

Years later, Mom said that they must have had rocks in their heads to let two young girls live in Houston, but it was good training in responsibility and accountability. I know both Klinka and I are stronger for the experience. Most weekends, we drove home to Brazoria County. It was fun to take our city friends with us and expose them to our country way of life.

Going to the University of Texas after graduation was like hitting the jackpot. Austin was still a small town, but the university had about 25,000 students. Klinka and I both joined Pi Beta Phi sorority, so we had a loving, close-knit sisterhood in the midst of that huge campus.

College challenged us, but we enjoyed ourselves to the fullest, at least until Klinka was injured in a terrible car accident that almost took her life. When she left school after her sophomore year, I really missed her. After fighting like cats and dogs the first twelve years of our lives, we had become best friends, as we still are today.

In my junior year I had a wonderful opportunity to spend the second semester abroad with my friends Maline Gilbert (McCalla), Nancy Beth Johnson (Roberts), and Lee Cullum. They were headed for France. My first choice would have been Spain because I wanted to become fluent in Spanish. But being too chicken to strike off by myself, I joined my pals for a Parisian adventure.[1]

We attended classes for foreign students at the Sorbonne and lived in a residential hotel across from the Luxembourg Garden on the Left Bank. Living on a shoestring didn't interfere with living large in Paris. Fresh, inexpensive food and good, cheap wine were available at the corner market or at Les Halles, the famous central market. For a few francs we could ride the Métro de Paris to anywhere in the city, visit museums, or attend the opera. And we picnicked in the Bois de Boulogne with sandwiches made from delicious French bread and peanut butter, a delicacy some GI friends bought for us at their PX.

One of the few inconveniences was bath time. Skipping a bath had been fun back when I was a child at a stock show. It was a lot less fun for six young women in Paris. Our tiny rooms had bidets, but no tubs, and the price for a hot bath down the hall was an exorbitant $1.50. The winter of 1960 was really cold, and I remember sleeping in my coat, wishing I could slip below the water in a steaming hot tub! When we were homesick for a hamburger, we had to pay $5.00 at the American Drug Store on the Champs-Élysées. That didn't happen very often, but when it did, it was worth every expensive bite.

The beauty of this ancient city along the Seine was stark in the winter, celestial in the spring. The sometimes violent student demonstrations against the Algerian conflict were jarring, and thought-provoking. The only other student demonstrations we Texas girls had ever seen were over the Texas-Oklahoma

---

[1] Sandra Brown from Houston and Ann Dubuisson (Sturgill) from Shreveport, Louisiana, joined us to form a happy gang of six.

football game. Even more sobering was our visit to Normandy Beach. As we approached, it was shocking to see so many bombed-out homes, barns, and commercial buildings, reminders of the violence of the combat in the weeks after D-Day. Most Parisians were a bit aloof, but the people of Normandy were as warm and friendly as my neighbors in Texas. These French men and women still remembered the American GIs with gratitude, and they made us feel very welcome.

When my parents encouraged me to go to Europe, it was to enlarge my understanding of the world. After my six months in France, their wishes had been realized. I learned a great deal about France and Europe in general, and about how large and interesting the outside world was. But most of all I learned to see my country more clearly and love it more dearly.

My only regret is that when I left I was dreaming in French. Fifty years later I can't say two sentences in that beautiful language—*Quel dommage!*

I didn't return to France for many years, but when I did in 1991, it was an extraordinary and unexpected experience. During my first visit to France, I was a Texas college girl, happy for *un baguette avec beurre de cacahuètes* (peanut butter on a baguette). This time I enjoyed *un banquet*—a multi-course work of art—at the Ministry of Foreign Affairs on the Quai D'Orsay. The host was French Foreign Minister Roland Dumas, and my dinner companion was my husband, the U.S. secretary of state.

Life certainly is unpredictable.

Chapter Three

BROKEN DREAMS
ༀ

JAMES O. WINSTON III WAS A DROP-DEAD HANDSOME DYNAMO AND
FORMER MARINE WHO COULD CHARM THE BIRDS OUT OF THE TREES.
HIS NICKNAME WAS JIMBO, WHICH PERFECTLY SYMBOLIZED HIS BOYISH, DEV-
IL-MAY-CARE SPIRIT. HE HAD DATED FRIENDS OF MINE SO I KNEW HIM BY
REPUTATION, BUT WE HAD NEVER BEEN INTRODUCED.

We met at an event I attended with my parents in June 1960. His parents
knew my parents, so he came by to say hello and ended up spending the whole
afternoon with us.

Just home from a junior-year semester at the Sorbonne, I had planned
to return to the University of Texas to complete a liberal arts degree in the
UT honors program. I was excited to rejoin my friends at the Pi Phi house.
Besides, I was going to be pinned—engaged to be engaged—to a great guy
from Dallas. Little did I know that after meeting Jimbo all these plans would
evaporate.

The summer of 1960 was a whirlwind. Jimbo wined, dined, and courted
me from the day we met, and it didn't take long for me to fall in love. When he

proposed in August, I was shocked. But I was so sure he was the man for me that I didn't hesitate to say yes. We were married two months later in Houston at St. Anne's Catholic Church, the beautiful old church where I had been baptized as a baby. Left behind were my senior year, my old beau, and the whispered warnings of several close friends. "He's a great date but don't marry him," they said. "He's a wild man."

Jimbo had a reputation for partying and drinking, but quite honestly, this didn't worry me; it appealed to me. The fact that he had sown his wild oats early made me think he had had enough of that life and was ready to settle down. After all he had asked me to marry him. Life with Jimbo promised to be exciting and fun for this straight arrow from Danbury.

Looking back, I think the dictionary should put my picture next to the definition of *naive;* within six months, I realized I had married a man with a serious drinking problem. He was good at heart and wanted to be married, but on his own terms. He just wasn't capable of accepting the responsibilities of a shared life.

Meanwhile, my sheltered upbringing had not equipped me to deal with this. To me, right was right and wrong was wrong. Why couldn't Jimbo just quit drinking and start living up to his potential? This young bride loved her husband but had no earthly idea how to help him.

The best of the good memories during this period were our children, precious and beautiful gifts. Elizabeth, our first, was born nine months and two weeks after our honeymoon. James O. Winston IV—known as Bo—was born twenty-one months later. Each time I saw my husband hold his newborn child, I dreamed that fatherhood would do what marriage had so far failed to do, but it was not to be.

I'll spare most of the details about our problems. They are private to our family. Later I learned, however, that these things, which seemed so dreadfully personal at the time, were in fact common in marriages touched by alcoholism.

Before Bo's first birthday things reached a crisis point. I packed my bags and left with the children to a location known only to my parents. Our marriage was in real trouble, and I was praying that this surprise move would get Jimbo's attention.

What happened next is probably familiar to those who have dealt with an alcoholic spouse. My husband promised to cut down on his drinking if I would just come home. He never admitted that he had a serious problem, and he wouldn't see a counselor, but I was desperate to believe him. Praying that Jimbo was serious about his promise to drink less, I returned home.

Will was born five and one-half years into the marriage. Once again, things didn't improve. Before Will's first birthday I again moved out, this time for three months.

A dear friend of Jimbo's family, Andrew Jackson Wray, took me to lunch one day. Jack Wray had been a notorious drinker in his youth, but through Alcoholics Anonymous he had regained control of his life. Speaking from his heart and experience, he helped me understand the realities of my situation. I don't remember his exact words but the message was direct:

"You did not cause Jimbo's alcoholism, and you are not responsible for it. No matter what you do, you cannot cure it. If your husband is unwilling to deal with his illness, you need to understand that it will kill him."

I was in tears—for Jimbo, for our marriage and our family—but my sense of guilt was greatly relieved. I had thought that if I loved Jimbo more or did things better, surely he would quit drinking. What I had just heard was what I had long feared. But what could I do? Life for me and the children had become so very difficult, at times almost unbearable. There seemed to be no way out. There was little prospect of restoring our marriage, and that realization led first to deep despair, and then to a slow acknowledgment that I had to do something that I had sworn I would never, ever do: get a divorce.

That's when I hit rock bottom.

Susan Blackshear Garrett was a born people-pleaser, a Goody Two-shoes who always—well, almost always—followed the rules. And if you followed the rules, things were always supposed to turn out right, weren't they? How could this be happening? What had I done wrong?

In this shattered state, I began to lose control and do things that were out of character for me. One evening my eight-year-old daughter did something that really upset me. I can't remember what it was, but I do remember that I became terribly angry and began screaming at her. Her little eyes got big, then she started to run. I chased her around the house—in and out of rooms, over furniture. What I might have done if I had caught her, I don't know, but fortunately she was too fast and too agile for that to happen.

When I stopped to catch my breath, I was horrified. How could I have flown into such a rage over nothing? How could I have come so close to really hurting the child I loved so much? I had wanted to kill her! Somehow I got the children to bed, then I went to my room, locked the door, and collapsed on the floor like a puppet whose strings had been cut.

I sobbed and sobbed. There were tears of sadness, of loneliness and disillusionment. In spite of the failed marriage, I had seen myself as a good, loving mother. This episode made me realize I was failing even at that.

My heart was wracked with despair and my body had all the symptoms that come with it—shortness of breath, tight chest, profound fatigue. I thought I understood how someone really could die of a broken heart.

"Oh God," I cried. "If You are really there, You have to help me! I can't go on like this!"

There was no blinding light or voice from above, but peace slowly settled into my heart, a peace I hadn't felt in ages.

An understanding washed over me, and I knew what I had to do. I had to seek God in earnest, not just take Him for granted. I had to find out if He was real. The next week I started going to a Bible study group at my friend Teddy Moody Hurd's house. That is where my real spiritual journey began.

Over the next weeks, months, and years, studying the Old and New Testaments, I discovered that my knowledge of the Bible was shallow and my faith secondhand. I knew the basics, but my wires were crossed about a very important point. I thought I had to *earn* my way into Heaven by doing good works. In my limited understanding, God gave us points for good conduct and took points away when we were bad. At the end, I thought, he would tally up the score and decide whether we were good enough for Heaven.

I was relieved to learn that I was wrong, that according to the Bible, we are saved *for* good works, not *by* good works. And that our salvation is a gift from God when we choose to believe and trust in Him, instead of ourselves or something else.

This message really was wonderful news to me. Before, I had viewed life as a minefield of dos and don'ts. I had lived hesitantly as I tried to prove myself and avoid making mistakes. The truth, however, is that we all sin and Jesus calls to repentance. "If we confess our sins, he is faithful and just and will forgive us our sins and purify us from all unrighteousness" (1 John 1:9). We are loved, and when we repent the Lord can turn the sins and lies of our lives into beauty and truth.

Coming from a loving family made it easier to understand a loving heavenly Parent. Still, it frightened me to think of making a real commitment to God, of putting my life in God's hands and saying "yes" to His control of how I lived. Because we are created with free will, it is our choice to follow God or not.

When I knelt by my bed to ask Jesus to be the Lord of my life, tears rolled down my cheeks. I remember this moment as if it were yesterday. I had a sense of joy but I was also scared to death. My fear was that with God in control I would probably never marry again. I was even worried that I wouldn't have any more fun. Maybe I would venture off as a missionary to some remote and dangerous land!

Since that broken moment on my knees, I have come to peace with many things, including the difficulties of my first marriage.

I believe that marriage is certainly critical to the stability of our families, the well-being of our children, and the health of our culture. We should do everything we can to strengthen marriages—in our own extended families, in our networks of friends, and in our laws and social norms.

And even though I have been divorced, I hate divorce. Children suffer terribly from the breakup of their parents' marriage and carry the wounds into their own relationships and marriages. The grown-ups also suffer. Being the child of my parents' solid (but far from perfect) marriage, I was especially traumatized by the failure of my own.

Three years after the divorce, I called Father Francis Monaghan, the priest who had married Jimbo and me, to discuss a possible annulment. This was a prerequisite to any hope that I might ever remarry in the Catholic Church.

Father Monaghan said he was sure we could get the marriage annulled because Jimbo had shown that he was incapable of following through on his commitment to marriage. But filling out the necessary paperwork completely undid me. Yes, Jimbo had failed to fulfill his role as a husband and father. Yes, we were both immature when we got married, and I was far from the perfect wife. But how could I deny our love for each other and our desire to have a life together? And what about our precious children? How could I use the church to read their father out of our family, as if our marriage had never existed? Where would that leave them?

I just couldn't do it. When I called Father Monaghan to tell him, he surprised me by saying he was proud of my decision.

As much as I despaired over my divorce, however, I never once regretted marrying Jimbo. Alcohol had robbed him of control over his daily decisions, and in time it would steal his life. Four years after the divorce he died of acute pancreatitis and cirrhosis. He was only thirty-eight. Still, his vitality and joie de vivre inspired me, and he opened up life to me in ways that changed me for the better—through happiness and suffering.

Our remarkable children are now loving, creative, and productive adults who have given me joy beyond description. In addition, I had the privilege of becoming part of the wonderful Winston family. I truly loved his mother, Ella, and his father, whom we called "Dear Father." Dear Father joined my dad to help nurture Elizabeth, Bo, and Will, and he also paid for their educations. Jimbo's brother, David, and sister, Libby, also joined Klinka, Jacko, and Bob to offer much-needed support. The Winston family ranch near Sabinal in South Texas was always a refuge for Elizabeth, Bo, and Will when they were young, and a valuable way for them to stay connected to their father's family. For all of that I will be forever grateful.

I never did go to Africa as a missionary, but I did visit there four years later…on my honeymoon. It seemed God had other plans for me when he sent a remarkable man into my life. I call him Jimmy. The world knows him as James A. Baker III. [2]

---

[2] Those who have known him a long time call him Jimmy. But in more formal settings he is called Jim, and that is how I will refer to him in the rest of the book.

Chapter Four

ACQUIRING SURVIVAL SKILLS

MY TRANSITION FROM BEING A DEPRESSED DIVORCÉE TO A BEAMING, ALBEIT HARASSED, BRIDE TOOK ABOUT THREE YEARS. HAPPILY, MY FUTURE HUSBAND JIM RESCUED ME FROM THE AWKWARD DATING SCENE AFTER A SHORT INTERVAL. IN THE BEGINNING, PERHAPS IT WAS JUST OUR COMFORT LEVEL WITH EACH OTHER AND OUR MUTUAL LONELINESS. HIS FIRST WIFE, MARY STUART, AND I HAD BEEN VERY CLOSE FRIENDS, AND HE AND JIMBO HAD BEEN SERIOUS HUNTING BUDDIES. OUR CHILDREN HAD GROWN UP TOGETHER. BEFORE LONG, OUR FRIENDSHIP AND RESPECT FOR EACH OTHER TOOK ON A DEEPER DIMENSION.

After a year of dating, we were silly enough in love to think of marriage. The idea of merging our two families took not only oceans of love, but also a ton of courage. Bonner Baker, Jim's mother, encouraged us to make the leap. It's no surprise that we both had reservations about marrying; between us we had seven children, ranging in age from seven to eighteen years. But on August 6, 1973, we took the plunge anyway, trusting our love and the grace of God, and committed to love each other "for better or worse."

Getting married was the right thing to do, but Jim and I made a huge mistake in how we did it. Because his Mother had been lobbying for us to tie the knot, we thought it would be fun to do it on her birthday. This would have been fine except that some of the children were going to be out of town then. Once we had decided to marry, we wanted to get it done. So instead of waiting until all of our kids could be there, we eloped.

After our secret four-day honeymoon to Jim's Rockpile Ranch near San Antonio, we came back to Houston to start our life together. We were happy as could be when we broke the news to our children, but they were surprised—*shocked* is a better word—when we told them what we had done. In hindsight, Jim and I certainly understand their unhappiness, and even anger. Just four years before, the Winston children had suffered through a painful divorce; a year later, the Baker boys had suddenly lost their beloved mother to cancer. Now the Winston mother and Baker father had left them out of an event that would profoundly affect their lives. It surprises me to this day that we were so insensitive. Love was certainly blind *and* deaf in this instance.

It was a rocky start, but at first things went well enough. We moved the Winston clan into the Bakers' two-story, three-bedroom house and divvied up rooms and bathroom rights. In September, the month after we married, we put three of our seven children in the seventh grade!

I still occasionally have nightmares about all the gyrations it took to maintain a modicum of order in our house. To keep up with all the clothes, our washer and dryer ran day and night; between loads I operated a nonstop car pool. Between trips to four different schools, doctor's appointments, and athletic and social events, I would descend on the grocery store for restaurant-sized portions of everything.

I'll never forget pushing an overflowing cart in the market six weeks after we were married and being stopped in the middle of the aisle by an attractive friend who had remarried several years before. She grabbed my arm and said, "Susan, isn't putting two families together just awful?"

I just stood there stunned, not knowing what to say. The honeymoon glow was still burning very brightly and—although I had seen some troubling signs of the terrors to come—I felt very confident about our recent merger. I can't re-member what I said, but I hope it wasn't anything too stupid like, "Everything is perfect," because six months later I found myself thinking, Dear God what have I done? This is worse than awful!

Of course, we experienced the little difficulties and adjustments that were to be expected. But the major trouble started when one of my stepsons declared open warfare on me and my children.

One day, at my wits' end and about to explode with frustration, I was desperately asking God for the umpteenth time to change this child and his attitude. Suddenly something I had been reading in Evelyn Christenson's book, *Lord, Change Me!*, popped into my mind. If we are dealing with a problem and nothing seems to work, she contends, then it is time to ask God if *"we"* need to change.

It was like a glass of cold water in my face.

You have got to be kidding, I thought. Despite this boy's most awful provocations, I have been fabulous. I've held my tongue when I've wanted to shout at him, and I've kept my hands to myself even when I wanted to pinch his head clean off. He's wrong; I'm right! He is the one who needs to change, not me."

I battled with all my might against this new idea. After many days however, I surrendered and faced my choice: I could stay in the rut of praying for our angry adolescent to change, or I could trust God's grace to change me to make this situation more bearable. When I was honest I knew I needed to love this hurting son more, not less, so for months I read a passage from 1 Corinthians 13 every day, sometimes three times a day, to remind myself what real love was—and is—from God's point of view:

> *Love is patient, love is kind. It does not envy, it does not boast, it is not proud. It is not rude, it is not self-seeking, it is not easily angered, it keeps no record of wrongs. Love does not delight in evil but rejoices with the truth. It always protects, always trusts, always hopes, always perseveres.*
>
> *Love never fails.*

Over the many months that I prayed to genuinely love our angry teenager, my feelings began to change. It reached a point where he would be cursing me and I'd put my arms around him and say, "I love you and nothing you do will ever drive me away." And I really meant it.

As I changed, the dynamics in our relationship began to change. It was not instant sweetness and light, but slowly, gently, unmistakably, the supernatural grace of God became evident in this relationship.

There is a lot more that I could say here, but I won't, at least not in detail. Our children carried a lot of burdens—death, divorce, the unexpected remarriage, learning to live with new step-siblings. Jim and I were molded by families with strong mothers and fathers, but the rebellious, antiestablishment spirit of the 1960s and 1970s seemed to have weakened our authority as parents. Add to that easy access to drugs and alcohol, and we had a recipe for trouble, the kind that can destroy young lives forever.

Some of our children suffered these troubles, but thanks to our faith, the support of family and friends, the help of gifted teachers and counselors, and their own perseverance and strength of character, all of them have grown into responsible, productive, and loving adults.

At Thanksgiving some years later, we all held hands around the table. Jim asked us to say a one-sentence prayer stating what we were grateful for. I began to get teary as, one by one, they gave thanks for the blessings in their lives.

Our once-rebellious son—the one who had vowed to break up our marriage—listened quietly to the others. He now had a family of his own, a good job, and responsibility for managing some family property. After all these years, his relationship with me, and mine with him, was strong and healthy. When his turn came, he said simply, "I thank God that my parents didn't give up on me."

It took more than ten years to fully work out our conflict. To say that this was a painful experience is an understatement, but it was one of the most profound lessons of my life. This process strengthened me, him, and—I suspect—the rest of the family as well. We got an up-close-and-personal glimpse of God's agape love—His "in spite of" love, described in the passage from 1 Corinthians.

This experience showed me in a very tangible way how God loved me—and my family—even when we rejected Him and went our own hurtful ways. I shudder to think what could have happened to our marriage if I had not had the comfort and guidance of my faith during this crisis.

The first two years of our marriage were the most difficult. After that, even though we still had many issues to resolve, the dust began to settle. I even began to think that our family was on the way to a semblance of normalcy.

Then in the summer of 1975 a call from Washington dropped a bombshell that stirred the dust up all over again. Rogers Morton, the friendly giant from Kentucky who served as President Gerald Ford's secretary of commerce, asked Jim to join the Ford administration as his under secretary.

It was an unusual invitation to say the least. Until 1970, Jim had been a Democrat and one who barely paid attention to politics. His friend George H. W. Bush never admitted it, but we know George passed Jim's name along to Secretary Morton. Now Jim was being asked to take a high-level appointment in a Republican administration.

My husband was thrilled. After eighteen years of practicing law at Andrews Kurth, he was restless and ready for a sabbatical.

I was a lifelong Republican activist, so—to a certain degree—I shared Jim's excitement. But I was also a wife and mother. The new job would require us to pull up our Houston roots and move to Washington. It would also demand a lot of Jim's time just as our new family was coming together.

In the end, I was wary, but game. Having an adventure in Washington could be a great experience. It would only be an interlude, I told myself. Jim would serve a few years, and then we would pack up and move back home.

Little did I know what the future would bring.

Chapter Five

ALL GOD'S CHILDREN
ↄ⅃ↄ

WITHIN A MONTH AFTER JIM WAS ASKED TO SERVE AS UNDER SECRETARY OF COMMERCE, OUR FAMILY WAS ON ITS WAY TO WASHINGTON, D.C. I REMEMBER WONDERING HOW IN THE WORLD WE COULD PULL THIS OFF, BUT FORTUNATELY TWO GOOD HOUSTON FRIENDS, SALLY CHAPOTON AND JOANNE LAWSON WILSON, LIVED THERE. WITH THEIR HELP I FOUND A TERRIFIC HOUSE TO RENT. IT WAS PERFECT: FURNISHED, LARGE ENOUGH FOR OUR FAMILY, AND ONLY ABOUT FIFTEEN MINUTES FROM JIM'S OFFICE AT THE COMMERCE DEPARTMENT. IT ALSO HAD A BEAUTIFUL BIG BACKYARD WE DIDN'T HAVE TO MOW: BATTERY KEMBLE PARK.

Sally and Joanne also clued me in about doctors and where the essential stores were located. Learning to navigate the crazy grid of Washington's streets was my first challenge. Traffic circles around statues of historic figures are beautiful, but there's no way for a stranger to drive through one of these merry-go-rounds without getting confused. Another problem is that streets in Washington don't just go north, south, east, and west: Many cut diagonally through the city.

When Pierre L'Enfant laid out the District in 1791, a major concern was how to defend the capital against a possible military invasion. Based on my experience, he succeeded! What army could get from here to there in D.C. without getting lost? This newcomer from Texas certainly could not.

Fortunately Jim and I were not lost about who was who in this complicated political town. A huge bonus was having our wonderful friends George and Barbara Bush living just minutes away. George was the head of America's Liaison Office to China and was soon to become director of the Central Intelligence Agency. Sunday lunches at the Bush home were a regular gathering place for delicious burgers and interesting new acquaintances.

Before Jim and I left Houston, I had been intimidated at the thought of what I would say to "all those important people" in Washington. Running a household for nine didn't leave much time for studying issues. But I soon discovered that people with big titles and important jobs generally don't want special treatment. Most are just normal people who work hard and want what is best for their families and their country.

Meanwhile Jim was really enjoying the challenge of working at the Commerce Department with Rogers Morton. As a former U.S. representative and chairman of the Republican National Committee, Rog knew government and politics inside out. He had also become a good friend and confidante of Gerald Ford when they served together in Congress. And like Jim, Rog was an avid outdoorsman.

Jim would come home with great stories. I loved hearing about his first visit to the Oval Office and about what a nice man President Ford was. He also told me about the president's young chief of staff, Dick Cheney, soon to become a good friend. Jim was particularly excited about working on the president's economic team with Bill Simon and Alan Greenspan, and about advising the president to veto a controversial labor bill.

In January 1976, we were surprised when Rog was named counselor to the president. President Ford wanted his help on the upcoming presidential campaign. This meant he would soon leave the Commerce Department and go to the White House; it also meant that Jim's job was in jeopardy. The incoming secretary would have the right to request his own man as deputy.

Jim thoroughly enjoyed serving as "acting secretary" at Commerce, but there were a few unsettled months as we wondered whether we would be going back to Texas or staying in D.C. In time, the president appointed Elliot Richardson, the distinguished former cabinet secretary and ambassador to the Court of St. James's, to serve as secretary of commerce. It was a happy day for us when we learned that Elliot wanted to keep Jim on as his deputy. Faster than I could believe possible, my husband was making a name for himself as the young lawyer from Houston who not only knew what needed to be done, but also knew how to get it done.

Of course I was delighted by Jim's success, delighted at how well our family had settled in, and delighted to live in such a beautiful city. Yes, it was easy to get lost in Washington, but its varied topography (gentle hills, parks, wetlands, and the Potomac), lush vegetation, tight architectural controls (height restrictions on buildings, for instance), and monuments and classic architecture offered an environment unlike any other in America. In the wind I could almost hear the whispers of all the great men and women who had shaped our remarkable country.

Still, one thing marred the lovely picture and always left me feeling sad and uneasy. To get to Jim's office on Fifteenth and E Streets, I had to walk past a number of people who lived on the streets.

Of course I had seen homeless people before, but never like this. Unkempt men and women, in need of baths, clad in foul-smelling clothes, a few without shoes, their feet wrapped with newspapers. Some panhandling. Others mumbling to themselves or sleeping fitfully on cardboard mattresses. A scene of loneliness and despair, of human beings stripped of all dignity.

Busy office workers, well-dressed government officials, bewildered tourists all walked by without acknowledging these people, looking past them as if they did not exist. I didn't acknowledge them, either. Part of me was afraid, even though another part of me wanted to help. But how? What do you do? Do you offer them money? Do you buy them a meal? And even if you do these things, how do you find them a better place to live than a hard sidewalk?

As I hurried by I saw myself in the faces of these unfortunate men and women, no different from me except for accidents of birth and good fortune. Not knowing what to do, I did nothing.

That was in 1975. When Jim and I went back to Washington in 1981 some of these same people, and many more besides, were still sleeping on the streets—particularly in the winter when the grates over the underground emitted their warm billows of steam. This time my friend Betty Roberts Boyle introduced me to food banking, which in turn led me to work with the homeless.

I met Betty when she moved to Houston in early 1979 with her husband Tom Roberts, the volunteer treasurer of George Bush's presidential campaign team. We became fast friends, as did our two-year-old daughters. Betty's gentle southern demeanor beautifully disguised her iron will!

She also knew a thing or two about food banking. Her mother, Elizabeth Boyle, helped start one of the first food banks in the country. Food banking, "America's Second Harvest" as the network of food banks was originally called, saves more than two billion pounds of groceries that would otherwise be destroyed each year, and feeds 25 million low-income Americans. We worked with John van Hengel, the visionary who had started the food banking movement in Tucson, Arizona, in the mid-1960s. Our efforts helped change government regulations to permit farmers, food distributors, and grocery chains to write off donations of food. We also had a hand in promulgating a Good Samaritan law to protect food donors from personal injury liability suits.

But we wanted to do more than help feed the homeless; we also wanted to help them find a place to live. By May 1983, Betty, Susan Cullman (political and civic activist), Eileen Evans (later a professor at George Washington University), Meg Graham (later a priest and rector of St. John's Georgetown Episcopal Church), Rabbi Martin Siegel (Columbia Jewish Congregation, Maryland), and I founded the National Citizens Committee for Food and Shelter (now the National Alliance to End Homelessness) as a 501(c)(3) corporation. We were a very small group intent on making a difference, but we had a very big learning curve ahead of us.

Our mission was to build bridges. On one side were homeless shelters and other service providers, always short of resources, always in crisis. On the other were concerned individuals, responsible companies, the bigger national nonprofit organizations, and dedicated government agencies that wanted to help, but didn't always know how. We saw our organization as the middleman—an agent to connect the needs of the care providers with the resources of those who could help.

Barbara Bush encouraged me to take advantage of Jim's position and high profile to help the cause. She also helped me by hosting meetings at the vice president's residence to educate cabinet wives about homelessness. Mitch Snider and Veronica Maz were among the advocates who spoke at our meetings; many cabinet wives joined the cause. We also created a business advisory council to tap into the corporate world, and inspired a campaign by the Ad Council to educate the poor on how to get food stamps.

Our first project was to solicit donations of surplus items from the federal government—cots, food, blankets, military-style rations, whatever would be useful—and distribute them to the nonprofit and faith-based organizations that helped people on the streets. Thanks to Caspar Weinberger, then secretary of defense, and one of his assistant secretaries, Lawrence Korb, the Defense Department steered load after load of surplus goods our way.

Secretary Margaret Heckler of the Department of Health and Human Services agreed to create an interagency task force on the homeless and to identify which shelters had the capability to distribute the goods. Thanks to this task force, tons of surplus supplies were made available to the shelters. Vacant military facilities were also rented for a dollar a year to nonprofits that housed the homeless. The Department of Housing and Urban Development made empty housing available for cities to use in their homeless programs.

The first years were very lean ones for our organization. Without the generosity of two Houston foundations, we never could have made it. Bob Mosbacher, Ron Walker, and others arranged for a large—and desperately needed—gift from the 1985 Reagan Inaugural Committee. Our board was a determined set of volunteers. Together with only a handful of staff members, we could at least make sure that some emergency needs were met.

If only this had been enough to solve the problem.

When we started in 1983 our nation had just suffered a deep recession. We believed that economic downturn was responsible for most of the homelessness we saw. Once the economy improved, we believed, our group could close its doors.

How naive we were.

The economy did improve—in fact, it boomed—but homeless numbers kept increasing. It didn't take us long to see that deeper, more systemic problems were at the root of this tragedy.

One difficulty in dealing with homelessness, then as now, was the lack of hard information about how many people lived on the streets, in shelters, or in intermediate housing. The best figures today come from a study—*"Homelessness Counts"*—published in January 2007 by the Homelessness Research Institute, a part of our National Alliance to End Homelessness. The report estimated that more than 670,000 men, women, and children were homeless in America in January 2007. A shocking 42 percent of them were "unsheltered," meaning that they lived on the streets. The Alliance also reported that more than 123,000 men, women, and children were chronically homeless—homeless for years on end.

Numbers are important, but numbers also tempt us to think of homelessness as an abstraction. It's more than that. It's about flesh-and-blood human beings. It's about men like Larry, injured on the job. When his meager resources ran out, he wound up on the street. Or about Mary Jo, who was proficient in five languages and taught at a well-known East Coast college before schizophrenia robbed her of the ability to function. For both Larry and Mary Jo, the bottom simply fell out of their lives. Alone and without help, they soon found themselves without a roof over their heads.

In the past, most of the homeless were single men. Today however, single men are just 48 percent. An increasing number are women and children. This is a consequence of what has been called the "feminization" of homelessness, predicted for a decade, now a sad reality.

In Houston, the number-one cause of homelessness for women is domestic violence at the hands of husbands or boyfriends, even fathers. When the women walk out the door, they often take children with them. This helps explain the high proportion of homeless families with children—a staggering 37 percent of the total nationwide, one-third adults, two-thirds children.

Think about it. Night falls, and about 165,000 boys and girls have no place to sleep except, if they are lucky, a shelter or temporary housing. How can they be expected to attend school regularly, much less do well? Imagine being the kid from the shelter, the kid who wore the same shirt or blouse today, yesterday, and the day before, the kid who will probably move before he or she can make friends. It's no surprise that depression is common among homeless children, and that their health and academic performance often suffer. What a horrible price our society pays when these children, through no fault of their own, fall by the wayside.

Some stereotypes about the homeless are true. Many are alcoholics or drug abusers. A good percentage are mentally ill or have the dual diagnosis of being substance abusers with mental illness. Too many are on the streets because public psychiatric institutions have been closed in favor of terribly underfunded community-based treatment programs.

These stereotypes hurt in two ways. First, they encourage some to treat homelessness as a moral failure or a condition that cannot be remedied. *How can we help these people if they won't quit drinking? Or take their meds? They should help themselves before they ask us to help them.* This perspective wrongly treats illnesses and other difficult circumstances as failures of character.

Second, these stereotypes distract us from the other realities about homelessness. Many homeless people are *not* substance abusers or mentally ill or even lazy. They're simply down on their luck, and for one reason or another they don't have the resources—family, friends, savings, a good job—to put their lives back together.

Sadly, people who cannot work or who work hard at low-wage jobs often cannot afford to buy or rent a decent house, apartment, even a room. And some who can *almost* afford a place to stay are thrown in the ditch by unexpected health problems, an automobile that needs a new water pump, or countless other personal or financial crises.

All sorts of factors contribute to homelessness, among them broken homes, teen pregnancies, drug abuse, and alcoholism. But the fundamental cause, I believe, is the ever-widening gap between low-end incomes and housing costs. Many people simply cannot afford any kind of housing. You and I couldn't afford it either if we were suddenly put in their places.

The National Alliance to End Homelessness started out just trying to meet emergency needs. As we learned more, however, solutions to the underlying problem became more apparent. And, the good news is now we know how to solve homelessness. Today, twenty-seven years later, under the effective leadership of Nan Roman, our little organization is no longer so little, and it has a much different task than the one we contemplated back in 1983. Our group now takes a much more sophisticated and comprehensive view of the problem.

Our bipartisan group now has more than 5,000 members. Most are housing and service providers and government officials, but we also have foundations, businesses, and caring individuals. We do research on homelessness, educate the public and corporations, and work with Congress and the administration. Our goal is to create better policies and programs to help the people who have nowhere to live.

The United States is blessed by great wealth, and large-scale homelessness here is simply unacceptable. These are all God's children—A mentally ill person eating from a garbage can. A homeless teenager offering his or her body to a stranger. A woman driven from her home by an abusive husband. Children whose poverty and lack of a permanent address destroy their future. Hardworking men and women who cannot afford even the smallest apartment for themselves and their families. Their lack of shelter shames us, and we must respond.

Well, I've certainly jumped ahead of myself. It's true that the homeless people in the capital city broke my heart in the mid-1970s. It was 1981, however, before my unfocused concern turned into a hard determination to get off the sidelines and help do something about the problem. Back in 1975 and 1976, I was still ferrying my children to school, still getting lost on the streets of D.C., and still adjusting to life as the wife of a government official. Then Jim suddenly took a big detour that changed our lives forever.

As I mentioned, Jim's mentor, Rogers Morton, went to the White House as counselor to the president in January 1976. That spring, Rog took charge of President Ford's election campaign. The arrival of Elliot Richardson as Jim's boss at Commerce proved to be a blessing, and he and wife Anne became delightful friends, as had the Mortons.[3]

The first political hurdle for President Gerald Ford in 1976 was to win the Republican nomination. Ordinarily that would not have been a problem for a sitting president. He was well-liked and widely respected, but he was no ordinary sitting president. His path from Congress to the vice presidency (to replace the disgraced Spiro Agnew), then to the presidency (to replace the disgraced Richard Nixon) was unprecedented in American history; Gerald Ford was our first unelected president. A nation traumatized by Watergate, a weak economy, and the sad aftermath of the Vietnam War was uncertain what to do next.

This encouraged Ronald Reagan, the former Hollywood actor and governor of California, to run against President Ford in the Republican primaries. Governor Reagan was a great campaigner, as we all knew, and it soon became clear that he had strong support around the country.

About that time, Jack Stiles, the man in charge of rounding up convention delegates for the President Ford Committee, died in an tragic automobile accident. At Rog's suggestion, I am sure, the president called on Jim to become the new delegate-hunter, and Jim accepted.

What a wild time—it was a tooth-and-nail fight all the way. Jim likes to say he is a "cross-the-t's and dot-the-i's" kind of guy, and that was exactly what was needed. His job was to keep all the Ford delegates in the corral while trying to round up a couple of hundred undecideds. When the opportunity presented itself, he would also try to cut stray delegates out of the Reagan herd.

To make things even more interesting, 1976 was the country's bicentennial year. I will never forget the celebrations: fantastic fireworks at the Fourth of July picnic at the White House; tall ships sailing majestically into the harbors in Baltimore and New York City; countless neighborhood parades; and fireplugs painted red, white, and blue. All in celebration of our nation's marvelous history.

Another monumental thrill for me that summer was attending my first state dinner, which honored Queen Elizabeth. Jim made sure some undecided Republican delegates were also invited. The elegance of the dinner in the White House garden, set with the fine antique crystal and china, the beautiful flowers arranged by volunteers, the stirring music of the Marine Band—these were the perfect backdrop for our royal guests. I enjoyed myself immensely, but poor Jim worked so hard courting convention delegates that he didn't have much time for fun.

I don't remember how the undecided delegates at the state dinner voted at the Republican Convention in Kansas City that August, but President Ford won the key test vote by only twenty-nine votes; he then won the nomination by 117 votes out of 2,257. This was the last contested convention in our nation's history. Jim came away with a sterling "can-do" reputation, both in the administration and in the press, which dubbed him "Miracle Man," his walkie-talkie code name at the convention.

Immediately after the convention, the Ford team flew to Vail to plan the fall campaign against Jimmy Carter. I went along for the trip and was there when the president did something totally unexpected: He asked Rogers Morton to become chairman of a blue-ribbon steering committee for the campaign, and named Jim the new chairman of the President Ford Committee.

For most of his life, Jim had not been involved in politics. Furthermore, he had been a Democrat, as many Texans were in those days. In 1970, however, he had crossed over to the GOP and run the Harris County campaign for his friend George H. W. Bush's unsuccessful U.S. Senate race against Lloyd Bentsen. Now, with only limited political experience in Texas and less than a year's experience in Washington, he was being asked to run a presidential campaign. What excitement! I couldn't wait to share the news with my parents, lifelong Republican activists.

President Ford started the campaign almost thirty points behind. He was a good man and a good post-Watergate president. Our whole family loved him, and we worked our hearts out in the campaign. Gradually, point by point, the gap in the polls began to close.

On election night, Jim and I gathered with other supporters at the Shoreham Hotel in Washington to watch the returns. The race was neck and neck; about 2: 30 a.m., however, it became apparent that Jimmy Carter would win. The popular vote favored the challenger by about 1.7 million out of 81 million votes cast, but the race for the Electoral College was much closer. A shift of fewer than 4,000 votes in Hawaii and fewer than 6,000 in Ohio would have elected Gerald Ford.[3]

This loss was a huge disappointment. In the sadness of defeat, however, I recognized a silver lining. Now we could take our family back to Texas.

---

[3] That night, Jim believed we had seen the closest presidential race of our lifetime. The Bush–Gore contest of 2000—remember Florida?—proved him wrong.

Chapter Six

KICKING AND SCREAMING
ༀ

BEFORE JIM AND I RETURNED HOME TO TEXAS AFTER THE 1976 PRESIDEN-
TIAL ELECTION, WE FLEW TO ITHACA, NEW YORK, TO SEE ONE OF OUR SONS AT
COLLEGE. THIS WAS OUR FIRST RELAXED LONG WEEKEND SINCE JIM HAD
JOINED THE PRESIDENT FORD COMMITTEE. WE HAD A GREAT VISIT WITH OUR
SON, AND OUR GET-REACQUAINTED TIME WAS PRODUCTIVE AS WELL. NINE
MONTHS LATER OUR BONUS BABY ARRIVED!

Because many of our kids were teens, Jim and I didn't tell them of
the pregnancy until two months before the birth. We expected them to be
embarrassed. "Mom, how could you!" "Aren't you too old?" A good girdle—
remember girdles?—helped me keep our secret. I even played tennis until the
seventh month.

When they found out, some of our children had misgivings about
the new arrival. Why did we need another character in the extended dramas
of our large blended family? Once the baby appeared on the scene, however,
they were goners. She was the most secure child I have ever known, and I am
certain it is because she has been so deeply loved by her seven siblings. She

helped knit our family more closely together.

Returning to Texas with a babe on the way was a blessing, but when Jim decided he wanted to run for attorney general in our state at the same time, I gulped. To him it was the most natural thing in the world. He had just run a national presidential campaign. How hard would it be to use the same skills to launch his own political career with a down-the-ballot statewide race in Texas? I have always believed in being active in politics, but Jim's timing really complicated our already complicated life.

Once we had been settled back in our home in Houston for a few months, I recovered my balance and sense of humor. With supportive family and friends all around, I lost my anxiety and began to be excited about this new political adventure. The hardest part of running for office is asking your friends to help financially, but Jim soon found plenty of enthusiastic supporters. Many volunteers also offered to work on the campaign, which made our job much easier. But not easy.

Running for office in Texas is like running a national campaign. With more than 268,000 square miles (and twenty-six media markets), Texas is larger than France or Germany. We have three of the ten largest cities in the United States (Houston, Dallas, and San Antonio) and six of the largest twenty-five (add Austin, Fort Worth, and El Paso).

Jim took the large media markets and assigned the medium-sized and small cities and towns to me. I don't recall the exact numbers, but the Lone Star state has more than 100 municipalities with at least 10,000 residents, and many of them are miles and miles from anywhere else.

In May, Jim handily won the GOP nomination. That's when the Baker campaign hit high gear. We bought the largest white Suburban we could find and painted *JIM BAKER FOR ATTORNEY GENERAL* in red, white, and blue on the side windows. Our baby was just eight months old, so we loaded her and her portable crib in back, filled the rest of the space with campaign literature, and off we went. I always had company—my campaign assistant Karen Jones, my sister Klinka, sometimes another family member or a friend. Over the next six months, I drove thousands of miles across Texas. We visited Corpus Christi, Brownsville, and McAllen; Amarillo and Lubbock; Waco, Fort Worth, and Abilene; Midland and Odessa; Beaumont, Port Arthur, and Orange; and

Tyler, Kilgore, and Longview, to mention a few. I really enjoyed being in these cities with their colorful histories and wonderful people.

Early on, my friend Anne Eastland, Democrat, corralled her pal Nellie Connally, wife of John Connally, former Texas governor (and former Treasury secretary under Nixon), to give me some campaign tips. Nellie said she always refused to give talks at coffees, and I soon discovered why.

My first campaign speech is seared into my memory. Friends of my parents arranged a large coffee in Lake Jackson, not far from my little hometown of Danbury. My wonderful Mom held my hand, prayed with me, and reassured me afterward that my shaky knees could *not* be seen through my skirt! My mouth also seemed to be full of cotton, and my brain refused to cooperate fully with my tongue. In time, these symptoms became less severe, but even after sixty-five coffees they never went away completely.

Over six months of campaigning, I also did many events with Jim. We were amazed at the friendly reception we received, even in East Texas, which was home to many Yellow Dog Democrats—people who, it was said, would sooner vote for a yellow dog than a Republican.

At that time, Texas was still a solidly Democratic state. Jim decided to run because most Texas voters, Democrats included, were fairly conservative, and Texas Democrats were on course to nominate a liberal candidate—young Price Daniel Jr. This was the chance Republicans had been looking for; unfortunately for us, the Democrats wound up selecting Mark White, a relatively conservative member of their party.

Much the same thing had happened to George Bush in his unsuccessful Senate campaign eight years earlier. He had geared up to run against a liberal incumbent, Ralph Yarborough, but wound up in a race with a moderate-to-conservative Democrat, Lloyd Bentsen—ironically, another friend of Jim's and mine.

When Mark White beat Price Daniel Jr, Jim's chances went south. We still believed we could win, but we knew the odds were against us. Still, we campaigned hard and with enthusiasm.

Our bonus baby has never met a stranger, probably because she started her life on the never-ending campaign trail. At each stop, strangers fed her cookies and competed to bounce her on their knee. She took her first steps in a newspaper office in Brownwood and kept wacky hours with no discernible ill effects.

But the demands of the campaign *did* have discernible ill effects on our household. The kids were good sports, but the unending parade of events, the frequent absences of Mom and Dad, and the constant focus on things political simply wore us out. It gave me a real appreciation for families that willingly endure the hardships of life on the campaign trail to make our political system work.

After giving the race our best shot, we were disappointed, but not surprised, when Mark White won the November general election. To decompress, Jim took me on a trip to the Florida Keys soon after the election. For two days we just slept. On the third day, the phone rang, and it was his buddy George H. W. Bush. I couldn't believe it when Jim hung up and said, "Well, Bushie is ready to start his run for the presidency."

I knew George had been talking to Jim about running, and they had already started an exploratory committee in Houston. But why couldn't George have just waited until Jim and I had recovered from the last election before asking him to start planning the next one? That is the one and only time in my life that I have been furious with that lovely man!

Jim agreed to help his friend, of course, which meant that the next few years were a blur. My husband traveled all over the country to help George line up support for the Republican nomination. When they started, George Bush was an asterisk in the polls and Jim soon became an asterisk at home. As punishment for his long and frequent absences, our baby would refuse to hug him for hours after he returned. Only after he had wooed her would she finally smile and throw her little arms around his neck.

He was not in my good graces, either. While he was gone I had to manage the family and the household without the support I needed. A few of our teenagers and young adults were having problems, and these were not just squabbles about blue jeans. There were problems with drugs and alcohol, problems requiring treatment programs, problems that needed the attention of the whole family. I really wanted to be a supportive wife, but after a year and a half of this, I was depressed and worn out.

In retrospect, I see that there was ample reason for me to be down. For too long I had rationalized away the sadness I felt because Jim—my husband, my lover, and my very best pal—was gone all the time. I had repressed my resentment and anger about being left alone to deal with the children and their problems.

Fortunately I was in Community Bible Study, a great interdenominational program, often called CBS. At my lowest ebb, our leader Julia Amelang scheduled a two-day retreat at her farm near Brenham; our topic for study was the Psalms.

King David, the author of the Psalms, loved life and loved God. In the most colorful and beautiful words, he sang praises to the Lord and shared his hopes and joys. More importantly for me, however—and for many others who have turned to the Psalms through the ages—he also vented his frustrations, fears, and anger.

"I am worn out and calling for help," he said in Psalm 69. Again and again he bared his soul and communicated with God in total honesty, never disguising his own pain, guilt, and confusion. The bottom line, however, was always the same: "I trust in you, O Lord."

Our little group talked about how humanity had been created with the capacity for powerful emotions—excitement, happiness, joy, and peace on one side of the scale; sadness, resentment, anger, and depression on the other. My pals helped me to see that I wasn't being honest with myself or with God when I didn't deal with my negative emotions. By repressing my feelings, I had become depressed.

My belief that a good Christian wife shouldn't feel angry and depressed was baloney. In fact, only now we are beginning to learn how important feelings are to our emotional and physical health. The medical community tells us that repressed fear, anger, resentment, and other strong negative emotions can make us very sick.

Being a supportive wife is still very important to me. But now, instead of stuffing my negative emotions into a box and closing the lid, I make a point of being honest about them. I also deal with them, not only when I pray but also when I communicate with my husband. It's a *good thing* I learned this when I did, because emotional honesty was one of my major survival tools in the tough town of Washington, D.C.

Jim moved back in January 1980 to run George H.W.'s campaign. I debated whether to go with him or to hold down the fort at home. Most of the kids were off at school, however, and in the end I knew I wanted to be with my husband. So I took a deep breath, loaded up our little one—who was deep in the throes of the terrible twos—and moved with Jim to a rented townhouse in Alexandria, Virginia, near the Bush headquarters.

As much as I dreaded the experience, it was a fine one. The toddler and I made some new friends at a little park down the road. We could walk to the grocery, and the days were relatively relaxed and carefree. A young friend, Melinda Allen (now Abell), joined us for a time, which made the experience even more fun. Jim was so openly appreciative of our being with him that I didn't even whine (out loud anyway!) about all the trips to the laundromat I had to make to keep the toddler in dry clothes during a snowy winter season.

George won the 1980 Iowa caucuses and did well in several other states, but by late May it was clear that the next nominee of the Republican Party would be Ronald Reagan. The Bush team stopped campaigning in May, and Jim and I scurried back to Houston. The timing was great. Our kids were coming home from school, and we were all looking forward to an uncomplicated summer.

Summer stayed uncomplicated for about one month, just long enough for Jim to acquire a black lab puppy, which the little one promptly named Rainbow Sunshine. Then came the GOP convention. Suddenly George Bush was the party's vice presidential nominee and Jim was recruited into the Reagan campaign organization. His assignment: to help plan strategy for the general election contest against President Jimmy Carter. This time Jim commuted back and forth to Washington, and I stayed home with the kids and our rambunctious puppy.

On election day, I flew to Los Angeles to join Jim. Riding in the taxi from the airport to the Century Plaza Hotel, I was excited to hear an afternoon newscast reporting that exit polls were heavily for Ronald Reagan. As GOP supporters gathered in the hotel ballroom a few hours later, it was clear that a Reagan landslide was in the making. It also appeared that Republicans would capture a majority in the United States Senate for the first time since the early 1950s. The party faithful at the hotel celebrated until the wee hours. What a difference from the subdued gatherings that marked President Ford's loss four years earlier.

For me, however, the joyous celebration stopped when I heard Mike Deaver and Stu Spencer—longtime Reagan insiders—talking to Jim, and talking seriously, about his serving as chief of staff in the Reagan White House.

Please don't misunderstand: The victory was glorious. It was wonderful for our fine candidates for president and vice president and their families, and wonderful for my parents and other Republican loyalists. It was also wonderful for Jim. In 1976, he had helped deny the Republican nomination to Governor Reagan. Now, four years later, he was a key member of the Reagan team.

But for me the victory was a double-edged sword. Delight and despair collided as I cried all night about the possibility of having to move back to Washington. I had been praying for several years for a break from our frantic lifestyle and our fragmented family situation. The crisis came the next morning when Governor Reagan officially asked Jim to serve in the White House. When I was with the president-elect I held myself together, but in truth I was completely undone.

Jim and I had been married only seven years, but it seemed more like seventy. We had had to deal with the complications of blending our families starting in 1973. But before we'd quite finished doing that, we had moved to Washington with Gerald Ford in 1975; a year later, Jim went on to manage Ford's presidential campaign. In 1977, I gave birth to our baby when I was almost forty years old, and the following year, Jim ran for attorney general of Texas. As soon as that campaign was done, he was tapped to manage George Bush's campaign for the party nomination for two years, and then he joined the Reagan campaign. Now we were looking at staying on the merry-go-round.

To say I was frazzled is an understatement. I was worn out, desperate for a break. God had been so faithful to me during all this, but I didn't want comfort; I just wanted to go home to Houston with my family and collapse.

Needless to say, that's not what happened. As I mentioned in Chapter One, Governor Reagan put his arm around me the day after the election and said I had nothing to worry about. He said he would make sure that Jim was home by six o'clock every night.

I knew better than that. But after many tears, much praying, and some kicking and screaming too, I finally made peace with Jim's decision and, I believe, God's plan for us. We would move to Washington, D.C., and remain there for fourteen years.

Our experiences in the Reagan and Bush administrations were amazing. These were the best of times and the toughest of times. For Jim to serve in such important positions was a privilege and an honor for him and for all of our family. But life at the top is tough anywhere, and it's *especially* tough in Washington. While I thoroughly enjoyed being the wife of a White House chief of staff—and after that, secretary of the Treasury and secretary of state— it was difficult coping with all the demands on my husband and our family.

When you work fourteen-hour days, six days a week, as Jim did, there is no time for family or anything else. I had learned to be honest, so I talked to Jim openly about the difficulties his professional obligations created for his family. On a good day he would say, "Honey, it will get better." On a bad day he would tell me, "Sweetheart, there is nothing I can do."

I was also peppering my prayers with complaints, but nothing changed. Finally in my quiet time one dreary day when I was gritting my teeth and nursing a sore toe from kicking the door extra hard, I came across a Bible verse Gen Bredesen had given me. She used it to deal with the frequent absences of her husband Harald, a noted Lutheran minister. The verse from Isaiah goes like this:

> *For your Maker is your husband—the LORD Almighty is his name—the Holy One of Israel is your Redeemer; He is called the God of all the earth. The LORD will call you back as if you were a wife deserted and distressed in spirit…*

That really hit home for me. Of course my head understood the demands of Jim's work and the importance of what he was doing, but my heart still felt deserted. After mulling this over for a while, I knew in my heart of hearts that I had a choice: I could stew about the fact that life wasn't as I wanted it to be, or I could let the unrealistic expectations go and depend on God's grace to help me through it.

Once I stopped fussing and started listening, there *were* solutions. The first was to accept reality: There was no way that Jim *could* play the role I wanted him to play. The second was to make an effort to build new and deeper friendships in Washington. Our extended family and hometown friends had given me enormous support in Houston; I recognized that I needed the same kind of help here.

It takes a great deal of energy and vulnerability to develop close "best friend" relationships, and I had not planned on doing that in Washington. I had thought, or rather hoped, we would be going home after two years. Now I understood that if I wanted to survive for the long haul, I had better do it.

And I did make wonderful, deep friendships with some great ladies, friends who could do things Jim couldn't do, such as play tennis, go to a movie, or take off for a few days to go to the beach. I also used my free time to help establish and run national organizations to address the plight of the homeless and to educate people about potentially violent and sexually explicit music targeted at young people.

I never doubted that the Lord had a plan for Jim in Washington, but looking back I see that he also had one for me. If I had spent all my time being miserable, I would never have had the energy to get involved in these projects. By helping others I also helped myself. The two advocacy organizations—and the friendships I developed with cofounders and supporters—have enriched my life and allowed me to grow in ways I would never have imagined.

Once I had a change in *my* attitude, there was an attitude shift in Jim as well. When I could talk about our situation without getting upset, he decided there *were* some things he could do differently. He started bringing his work home on Saturdays, he modified his schedule to attend important school functions, and when he played golf, he played with me, even though I was a beginner who didn't keep score.

My desire to "write the script" negating a second Washington journey was understandable, but I am thankful that my prayers were not answered. Our Washington life, while far from perfect, was fascinating and life-enhancing. Today all the children appreciate the value of this sojourn and the opportunities it afforded them, in spite of the complications. And I must say, once we left the center of power, life seemed mighty tame.

Chapter Seven

WIFE OF...

ᴄᴀᴏ

THE SURVIVAL SKILLS I NEEDED AS THE WIFE OF A HIGH-PROFILE GOVERN-
MENT OFFICIAL RANKED SECOND ONLY TO THOSE I NEEDED A FEW YEARS
EARLIER TO PUT OUR SEVEN KIDS TOGETHER IN A THREE-BEDROOM HOUSE!
FLEXIBILITY, PATIENCE, ENDURANCE, AND A GOOD SENSE OF HUMOR TOPPED
THE LIST.

As White House chief of staff Jim oversaw everything that went on in the
West Wing—who saw the president, what went into the president's in-box,
and what went on the president's calendar. He also handled relations between
the White House and Congress and between the White House and the media.

The president called the plays on Reaganomics, national defense, and other important issues, but Jim often played quarterback. He would usually leave
home at about seven o'clock in the morning and often not return home until
after nine thirty at night, even on some weekends.

The president meant well when he told me in November 1980 that members of his administration would be home for dinner every night, but it was
just not to be. The job demanded more, and Jim, the perfectionist, would not

have been happy—or nearly as effective—if he hadn't given more.

Still, the hours weren't the worst of it. The job was also emotionally draining. Day after day, the chief of staff was a lightning rod for political criticism aimed at the administration. At times Jim was also caught up in internal squabbles at the White House—sometimes over policy, sometimes over turf. Constant controversy and turmoil would be hard on anyone, and they were certainly hard on him.

For the "wife of" and our family this translated into not having as much time with Jim as we wanted. And our limited hours with him were defined by his need to recharge his batteries and his constant concern about what was going on at 1600 Pennsylvania Avenue.

I think every Washington "spouse of" would agree that government officials and their families pay a big price for their public service. Having an important position is a great honor, and there are perks (though not as many as people might think). But the cost is high—for the officials and their families, particularly the children.

Some people disagree, but having lived through it, I think we get good value from our high-level government servants (regardless of party). Most of them put in twelve-to-fourteen-hour days, and weekends as well, for salaries far lower than they could earn in the private sector.

As for the perks, the glitz and glamour *were* a form of compensation, both for Jim and me. It *was* a thrill to see important events from front-row seats, to meet celebrities and world leaders, and to play a role in the exciting history of those years.

As chief of staff, Jim always traveled with the president. There were rarely seats for wives in the traveling party, except of course for the first lady. Most of my experiences with Jim's White House travels were secondhand. I heard the details in his telephone calls from the road or after he arrived home.

In 1982, however, Ursula Meese, Carolyn Deaver, and I were invited to attend the G7 economic summit in France. (We were "wives of" the White House "troika" of the time—Ed Meese, Mike Deaver, and Jim.) It was to be a fabulous trip. On the way to Paris, we were to have dinner with Queen Elizabeth in her private quarters and spend the night in Windsor Castle. The next day we would go to Versailles for the three-day summit. On the way home we would stop in Rome for an audience with Pope John Paul II.

Talk about bad timing: The dates of the trip collided with the junior high graduation date of one of our sons. In situations like these there are no options. Jim had to go; I stayed home and went to the graduation.

Happily the next year I *did* go to Ireland and England on a presidential trip, but I flew a commercial flight, as there was no room on Air Force One. Even if there had been, spouses who rode the president's plane had to pay first class plus a dollar. The money I saved by flying coach class bought a bundle of Christmas gifts that year.

In the first two years of the Reagan administration, Jim and I went to Camp David many times. This rustic retreat has been a refuge for all presidents since Franklin Delano Roosevelt, and it was a super place to unwind.

Generally we would have dinner with the Reagans and other guests, and later watch a movie. Our little girl was only three when we first dined with the president and Mrs. Reagan at Camp David. Jim and I were holding our breath about what she might say or do, but she was quiet and well-behaved…until…

Suddenly she disappeared! All I could see were her blonde curls under the table cloth. "What's the matter?" I asked quietly. With her lower lip quivering, she answered, " I dropped my bean!"

Another highlight was traveling to California with the Reagans when Queen Elizabeth visited in 1983. This was turnabout for the president's visit with the queen the year before—the trip I missed.

The Reagans' ranch house was often called the Western White House, but it was modest, only about 1,500 square feet in size. Reporters couldn't understand why the president had invited the queen there, and he was a little miffed by the suggestion that she may have been a reluctant guest. In fact, Queen Elizabeth had asked to see Rancho del Cielo.

Unfortunately the weather did *not* cooperate. The worst torrential rains in years descended just as the royal entourage arrived. The drive up the narrow, winding road was dicey, with streams overflowing their banks. When we finally reached the Reagans' Shangri-la, their lovely view of the Pacific was completely shrouded in fog.

Nancy Reagan served Mexican food, which thrilled Jim and me, but the cuisine was a little confusing to the queen. The president told her to eat the taco like a sandwich, which she did. And the taco did what tacos always do: It fell apart! Still, the event was a great success.

A few days later the royals treated the Reagan troops to a wonderful evening aboard the royal yacht *HMY Britannia* in San Francisco harbor. The vessel was huge, longer than a football field. Before dinner, guests were treated to a tattoo, a ceremonial military exercise on the dock. The decor of the ship was like an English country house with lots of chintz and mahogany furniture.

The Reagans reciprocated with an "unofficial" state dinner for the queen in San Francisco's de Young Memorial Museum and the Asian Art Museum in Golden Gate Park. The guest list included our good friends from Texas, Anne and Tobin Armstrong. In the 1970s, Anne was the much-loved ambassador to the Court of St. James's.

The queen's visit generated a lot of a favorable press, which was a delightful turn of events. Day in and day out, one of the toughest aspects of public life is dealing with the media. For prominent government officials, negative stories are inevitable. Fortunately, Jim didn't get upset about them the way I did.

It used to drive me up the wall when reporters got their facts mixed up, wrote about Reagan loyalists who accused Jim of derailing the Reagan Revolution, or questioned Jim's integrity. I often urged him to write letters of rebuttal, but he rarely did. "Never pick a fight with people who buy ink by the barrel," he would respond. Complaining would just keep the negative story alive one more day, he said, and of course he was right.

In general, though, Jim had good relations with the press, better than most others in the administration. He was good about talking to reporters off the record to give them background information. That kept the stories focused on the president, and not on him.

There were a few funny incidents with the press as well. My favorite was a mock report in 1984 by CBS White House correspondent Lesley Stahl. Jim was in his fourth year as chief of staff, and everybody knew he was burned out and wanted a change.

Lesley reported on the closed-circuit White House television channel that James Baker was about to resign to deal with a serious health problem—anorexia nervosa, the eating disorder most often associated with young women. Her practical joke was so good that when it first came on the screen, our team momentarily thought it was a real network piece.

Jim knew that Lesley was negotiating for a job as moderator of *Face the Nation,* the CBS Sunday interview show. So he called CBS president Tom Wyman and enlisted Tom's help in settling the score.

As agreed Tom then called Lesley and chewed her out. "Have you taken leave of your senses?" He said her lack of good judgment had given him second thoughts about *Face the Nation.* Tom kept her dangling a few days, then told her it was all a joke.

It may have all been done in fun, but I know that Lesley's Stahl's fake story had a kernel of truth: Jim really wanted out of the White House. Based on the advice of other former chiefs of staff, he had signed on for two years. Only his loyalty to the president kept him there longer.

During his fourth year as chief of staff, he rarely smiled, much less laughed. The stress and intensity of the position and his own sense of responsibility were wearing him out.

In late 1984, Treasury Secretary Don Regan suggested that he and Jim trade jobs—Jim to Treasury, Don to the White House. I thought it was a grand idea! That switch gave Jim a whole new lease on life. And for this "wife of," the change was like dying and going to heaven—I got my husband back.

At Treasury, Jim was in charge of his own schedule, and he was able to deal directly with important public policy issues. At the White House the president set policy, and Jim and others in the administration worked to implement it. At Treasury, even though he coordinated his actions with the White House, he was the boss. That first year, for instance, he negotiated an agreement with finance ministers in other countries to stabilize world currency exchange rates.

In 1985 and 1986, Jim also worked closely with Congress to simplify the federal income tax system. The tax reform bill of 1986 was one of President Reagan's—and Jim's—greatest accomplishments. It did away with many loopholes and reduced federal income taxes to the lowest rates in decades. Patrick Moynihan, a Democrat and a good friend of Jim's, said it was the "most ethical" thing the Senate had done while he served there.

Treasury also revived the spirits of this "wife of." As a cabinet spouse I could travel with my husband when my schedule allowed, which was often. By 1985 all our children except the youngest had graduated and were out of the nest. I made trips to China, Korea, Morocco, and many other exotic places. Jim worked on these trips, but I had few official duties, so I could see the sights. It was the best of all worlds.

In August 1988, Jim left Treasury to run the presidential election campaign for our dear friend, George H.W. Bush. The first announcement president-elect Bush made after his November victory was to name Jim secretary of state.

Serving as secretary of state was an extraordinary experience for Jim. To this day, he thinks it was the best job he ever had, and the best job in government.

As "wife of," I had few official duties at the White House or at Treasury, but I was inundated with them at the State Department. Almost every week, often several times a week, I would host official teas, coffees, or luncheons, or stand in a receiving line and attend an official dinner.

Each event was more or less formal. This required some mental adjustment for me. My favorite lunch is a sandwich or salad with good friends, all of us wearing jeans. It surprised me how much I enjoyed my new dress-up role.

One secret to my happiness was the amazing protocol department that did the hard work of pulling the events together. Another secret was the fabulous setting, the beautiful living museum of American antiques on the eighth floor at the State Department.

First Kay Bruce from Houston, then Carolyn Deaver, and finally Mary Claire Shipp Murphy—each did a marvelous job working with the U.S. chief of protocol, Ambassador Joseph Verner Reed, to make every event and every detail perfect. As assistant chiefs of protocol for ceremonials, they helped select the flowers and the menu (with tasting sessions for big events). They also recruited interesting people for the guest lists, found generous donors for the wine, and seated everybody in the right place—the hardest task of all.

These social events generally honored a visiting head of state, a foreign minister, another dignitary, or the principal's spouse. Occasionally Jim would honor a visiting head of state with a luncheon for 120 to 150 guests, but he preferred smaller working lunches. He liked to talk business while he and his guests enjoyed their meal.

One of the most memorable formal luncheons took place on November 9, 1989, and honored Corazon Aquino, president of the Philippines. Just before the dessert course, Jim stood up and announced that the Berlin Wall had fallen. What an amazing moment!

Jim spent almost as much time in the air as he spent in his office at the State Department. In his three years and seven months in office, he logged more than 720,000 miles. That's the equivalent of almost twenty-nine times around the globe. His staff made a T-shirt with the logo, "James A. Baker's Round-the-World Tour." On the back, it listed sixty-three countries from Albania to Zaire, "and still counting…" The final count was more than ninety countries.

Having a young teenager often kept me at home, but I still made about 60 percent of the trips. We were very fortunate to have some wonderful young women who lived with us during the fifteen years we were in Washington.[4] They enhanced our lives and provided the flexibility and the continuity that allowed me to attend myriad "must-do" events and to travel as well.

When we were on the road, Jim was so busy with meetings that he could never see the sights. After fulfilling my official duties, I would visit the historic quarters of the cities and the local markets, and walk the streets to soak up the atmosphere. Jim enjoyed getting a sense of the local culture through my eyes.

On the first official trip after Jim was sworn in at the State Department, we traveled to all sixteen NATO countries in nine days. That was a real baptism by fire, and it prepared us for what lay ahead. During this trip Elspeth Howe, wife of British Foreign Secretary Geoffrey Howe, impressed on me how important it was for the wife of a man in Jim's position to be involved in her husband's foreign travels.

Later, Jim and I went to places I had never heard of before, such as Brunei on the northern coast of Borneo. Sultan Hassanal Bolkiah had two wives, and each one entertained me separately. Queen Saleha, the first wife, lived in a palace with more than 1,700 rooms—a beautiful, but hardly cozy, building that also housed government offices. It was an elegant but imposing structure. The second wife, Queen Mariam, lived in a palace that looked like a Southern plantation in the rolling hills of Kentucky.

---

[4] This great support system consisted of Robin Prichard, Julie Bogaard Ginader, Eleanor Montague, Carla Bogaard, Sue Fash, Karen Schriever Lammerding, Virginia Woodward, Rebecca Pogue Brignoli, Emily Walker Kicklighter, and Lisa Margraves.

The two queens were wonderfully warm and hospitable, and gave me lovely (and expensive) gifts that I couldn't keep. Everywhere we went, our hosts gave us presents but we could only keep those valued under $180. To keep a more expensive gift we had to buy it from the government at a price set by an appraiser, whose fee we also had to pay.

Gift-giving is an important custom in many cultures, but less so in the United States. Jim and I would receive the most lavish gifts, but our gift budget was very limited. One of my most challenging jobs was to find interesting and inexpensive presents for our hosts and hostesses. We tried to select items that were unique to our country—such as Native American or craft items—or objects that came from a unique American store such as Steuben Glass or Tiffany's.

Serving at the State Department during this period had many thrilling aspects—watching the Soviet Union open up under Mikhail Gorbachev, experiencing the fall of the Berlin Wall, and witnessing the flowering of independence and democracy in Eastern Europe and Central Asia. In December 1991, the Soviet Union ceased to exist. The Cold War was over.

I saw the events in Eastern Europe as providential. From the day he became Pope in 1978, John Paul II spoke and worked tirelessly against communism and for religious freedom and independence for those behind the Iron Curtain.

Some credit the Pope's pilgrimage to his native Poland as pivotal to the liberation of Eastern Europe. He told the long-suffering Poles they had been chosen for a grand role in history, and he urged them to reconnect with their centuries-long Christian heritage. "You must be strong, my brothers and sisters!" he told worshippers at an open-air Mass. "You must be strong with the strength that faith gives!"

By some accounts, the pope inspired and strengthened the Solidarity movement, which forced Gorbachev to try to reform communism. That in turn set in motion the events that ended communist rule.

On June 7, 1982, the pope met privately in the Vatican library with President Reagan. This meeting was the day after the G7 economic conference in Paris—the very trip I had hoped to make, but had to cancel. Both the president and the pontiff had survived assassination attempts the year before, and each believed God had spared him for a reason. Reporters later said the two men agreed to work together below the radar to support the Solidarity movement in Poland and to promote freedom for all of Eastern Europe.

Through the 1980s, many were praying for the Iron Curtain to fall. There are even stirring accounts of fervent prayer sessions in Eastern Europe and Germany before the Wall fell and before Czechoslovakia, Hungary, and their neighbors declared independence.

Jim and I first visited the Soviet Union in May 1989, four months after President Bush took office. At that point some in the administration were not sure that the Soviets were serious about opening up. What we found in Moscow was a genuine desire for change, but no good plan for how to manage the process of change. Gorbachev was not trying to end communism; he was trying to reform it. That took a great deal of courage. What was lacking was a clear vision of what reform meant.

Our relationship with Mikhail and Raisa Gorbachev was delightful, but we developed an even deeper friendship with Eduard Shevardnadze, the Soviet foreign minister, and his wife Nanuli. Eduard was a strong, gentle man with a ready smile and silver-white hair. Nanuli had a larger-than-life personality with an elegant bearing to match. Even though every word we said had to be translated, the four of us developed a deep and trusting relationship. I am still amazed that such a thing was possible. Without that trust, Jim believes progress on ending the Cold War could have been much slower and, perhaps, less peaceful.

In September 1989, Jim invited Eduard and Nanuli to a ministerial summit in Jackson Hole, Wyoming. Before that, Soviet officials could not travel more than twenty-five miles from Washington, D.C., New York, or San Francisco. U.S. diplomats were subject to similar restrictions in the Soviet Union.

The trip gave Eduard, Nanuli, and the Soviet delegation a flavor of the American West and introduced them to people outside the D.C.–New York City axis. Working in the shadow of the beautiful Teton Range also expanded everyone's horizons. Jim and Eduard had a photo-op fishing trip, but real breakthroughs occurred on arms control and other U.S.–Soviet issues.

At the closing dinner Jim gave Eduard a pair of cowboy boots stitched with Soviet and U.S. flags and with the Soviet foreign minister's initials. Eduard gave Jim a much more meaningful gift—a beautiful enamel painting of Jesus teaching the people. "See, even we Soviets are changing our world-view," he said.

Other signs of change were evident on a European trip Jim and I had made with President Bush and Barbara two months earlier. We stopped off in Hungary (where the government was rapidly democratizing) and Poland (where thousands of people lined the streets to greet our motorcade).

Should the president have lunch with the communist government of General Jaruzelski or with Lech Walesa, leader of the Solidarity movement, which had just won a round of "semi-free" elections? The president insisted that both sides be included. Because tensions were so high, many were betting that *no one* would show up. But guess who came to lunch? Everyone.

One Bush staffer asked a Solidarity member how it felt to share a meal with the men responsible for putting him in prison. The future of Poland was too important to let past grievances stand in the way, the Polish guest replied.

Twelve months later the world was a different place. The Berlin Wall had fallen. Lech Walesa was the new president of Poland, and free elections had been held in East Germany. East and West Germany would soon peacefully reunite as a member of NATO. One former communist country after another was declaring independence from the Soviet Union.

With everything going so well, what a shock it was in August 1990 when Saddam Hussein suddenly invaded Kuwait. Middle East experts in the administration, the Soviet Union, and elsewhere thought Saddam had moved troops to the border for leverage in his talks over unpaid Iraqi debts, a disputed oil field, and other matters. The actual invasion caught the world off guard.

When the news broke I was in the air with Jim en route to Mongolia. That rugged country, sandwiched between China and Russia, had just completed the first democratic election in its history. My husband wanted to congratulate and encourage the people of Mongolia, the first communist country in Asia to embrace democracy and free markets.

We had planned to make a brief excursion to the Gobi Desert after the meetings. Jim wanted to see the exotic animals of Mongolia and the wild expanse of the desert that so few Westerners had visited.

The invasion changed everything. Immediately after meeting with Mongolia's new leaders, he cancelled the balance of our trip, and it was wheels up for Moscow. At the airport there, Jim and Eduard Shevardnadze issued a joint statement condemning the invasion. This was an historic first—the two Cold War adversaries acting together. What made this even more remarkable is that Iraq was a Soviet client state.

In Jim's mind this joint statement, even more than the fall of the Berlin Wall, signaled the beginning of the end of the Cold War. By coordinating their response, the two superpowers proved that civilized nations could cooperate to promote the rule of law in international relations.

Jim spent the next five months traveling to build an international coalition to eject Iraq from Kuwait. When war came the world was remarkably unified. Fighting on the ground lasted exactly 100 hours. Hostilities ended on February 27, 1991, with the Iraqis fleeing toward Baghdad.

Shortly after the war, I traveled with Jim to the Middle East. As we flew into Kuwait City, we could see the burning oil wells, hundreds of them, that Saddam Hussein's troops had set on fire as they fled. We also saw what has been called "the highway of death" on which Saddam's tanks, personnel carriers, and other vehicles had been destroyed by coalition aircraft. Jim called it a scene "straight from Dante's *Inferno*." The smoke was so dense that our pilots were uncertain at first whether they could land.

While Jim met with government officials I visited with about fifty Kuwaiti women who had experienced the horrors of the war. They told stories of looting, torture, and murder. Hospitals had been stripped of equipment. Women had been raped and abused. Their husbands' mutilated bodies had been thrown in their front yards. Sons had been abducted, and mothers still had no idea where they were. (Many are missing to this day.) One woman had a relative whose breasts had been cut off.

"I have never liked the United States," one woman told me frankly, "and yet you have come to our rescue even when our neighbors would not. We will never forget the debt we owe you."

We prayed together, Muslim and Christian, that God would heal the wounds of families and that torn nation, and that men and women of goodwill would work together for peace so generations to come would not suffer the devastation of war.

After Jim and I left Kuwait we traveled to Riyadh. The Saudi foreign minister, Prince Saud al Faisal, hosted us for dinner in his home, along with the ministers of some other Arab countries and their wives. This was the first time women had been invited to an event of this nature, I was told. The stars of the evening were General "Stormin' Norman" Schwarzkopf, commander of the coalition forces, and other leaders of the military campaign that drove the Iraqis out of Kuwait.

What I remember best, however, were our hosts' compliments about the American troops. Invading Iraqi soldiers had abused the Kuwaitis in every way imaginable. Several at the dinner said they were fearful of how the Americans—mostly non-Muslims—would behave when they arrived. What happened is that the young Americans were models of discipline and decorum. What a joy it was to hear our soldiers, sailors, and airmen praised in this way!

This new atmosphere of goodwill inspired President Bush and Jim to organize a regional conference to promote peace between Israel and her Arab neighbors—Syria, Lebanon, Jordan, and representatives of the Palestinian people. Hostile neighbors negotiated face to face, breaking the ancient taboo against Israelis and Arabs talking peace with each other. Other Muslim countries, including Saudi Arabia, joined in multilateral talks. The mere fact of the meeting itself was historic.

Within three years, Jordan and Israel had signed a peace treaty and Israel and the Palestinian Liberation Organization had signed the Oslo Accords—a first step that, sadly, has yet to lead to real peace between Palestinians and Israelis.

Then in 1991 came the turmoil in Yugoslavia. When the Soviet Union began falling apart, long-suppressed tensions flared, much of the conflict fueled by religious and ethnic differences. Separatists in Slovenia, Croatia, and Bosnia broke away from Serbia. Civil war was imminent.

The Europeans wanted to take the leadership role in resolving this crisis. The U.S. had had its hands full with Kuwait, the Middle East, and other issues, and was all too glad to defer to Europe. In June, however, Jim (with me in tow) did travel to Belgrade to try to persuade local leaders against a violent breakup of Yugoslavia.

While we were there, Janja Loncar, wife of the Yugoslavian foreign secretary, hosted a small luncheon for me. She invited a cross-section of women leaders—a poet, a television personality, a doctor, a businesswoman, an academic, a lawyer, and others. They represented all three major local religions—Islam, Catholicism, and Orthodox Christianity.

No one wants civil war, the women said, but war is inevitable. I couldn't understand why. "Two hardheaded mountain men are determined to fight it out," they replied—referring to Slobodan Milosevic, president of Serbia, and Franjo Tudjman, leader of the Croatians.

Indeed, war came, and the world could not prevent it. Neighbor began to kill neighbor; no one was exempt. Not civilians, women, children, or old people. Before it was over, these two misguided men—Milosevic and Tudjman—had triggered a conflict that would kill tens of thousands and had again made "genocide" a household word.

That luncheon and the horrible bloodbath that followed reminded me of what an incredible blessing it is to live in the United States. All religions are welcome; we generally respect ethnic differences. And even when we disagree vehemently with the politics of our president or other elected officials, we speak through the ballot box, not down the barrel of a rifle.

This "wife of" is deeply grateful for these blessings. And I am doubly grateful for the opportunities I have had to support Jim in his work, for the wonderful people I have met along the way, and for the front-row seats my family and I occupied during this remarkable period of history.

Chapter Eight

EXPLETIVES NOT DELETED

"MOMMA, WHAT'S A VIRGIN?"

That question changed my life.

It came from our young daughter in late 1984. She was all of seven years old, still playing with her Cabbage Patch doll.

"Why do you ask, honey?"

"There's this song on the radio," she said, mimicking what she had heard. "*Like a virgin, touched for the very first time. Like a virgin…*"

"What does it mean, touched for the very first time?"

I was speechless.

Who was robbing our little girl of her innocence and pushing sexual awareness on her when she wasn't prepared for it? That someone, I would quickly learn, was Madonna, a twenty-six-year-old singer who was making a name for herself—and bucketloads of money. "Like a Virgin" was her big hit at the time. "*Gonna give you all my love, boy…been saving it all for you…feels so good inside…*" were just a few of the lyrics.

Thanks to a new medium called MTV, her music videos were being piped into homes across the country as part of the basic cable service. I may not have known who she was but, as I would soon learn, almost every kid in America did.

As a teenager I had danced to rock and roll—Buddy Holly, Elvis, Fats Domino—and I really liked it. I also understand that adult themes have a place in art, fiction, drama, cinema, and music. There have always been suggestive lyrics, but they were for grown-ups, not, in my opinion, prepubescent children. I knew I had to be vigilant about movies and TV shows, but I had thought music was safe.

About the same time I found out that Pam Howar and Sally Nevius, two friends who also had young daughters, were upset over similar experiences. As we began listening more carefully to what was out there, we quickly learned that "Like a Virgin" was tame compared to some other songs.

Like other songs glorifying violence, particularly against women. Songs glorifying mindless sex, rape, incest, bestiality, and drug and alcohol use by teenagers. Songs glorifying suicide and satanism.

What we heard made us fighting mad. We decided we needed to alert parents and educators about the growing popularity of what we called "porn rock."

Sally, a lovely and determined Southern belle, was a former dean at Mount Vernon College in Washington, D.C., and wife of a prominent D.C. councilman. Pam was a businesswoman and wife of a major real estate developer. By this time, I was deeply involved in working with the homeless, and Jim had just moved over from the White House to serve as Treasury secretary.

As Sally, Pam, and I thought about what to do, my political antennae alerted me. We were all identified with one political party. But porn rock was not a partisan issue; it was a human issue, an issue of values and childhood development, an issue for Democrats as well as Republicans.

So in the spring of 1985 I visited another friend, Mary Elizabeth Gore—known to everyone as Tipper. She was an energetic young mother with four children, a gifted writer and photographer, and a Democrat. Her husband, Al Gore Jr., had served in the House and was a first-term U.S. senator from Tennessee.

Tipper was a serious fan of rock n' roll; in high school she played drums in an all-girl rock band. She, too, had awakened to the new reality of porn rock when her oldest daughter, Karenna, then eleven, brought home a popular 1984 album titled *Purple Rain* by a twenty-six-year-old singer named Prince. When Tipper sat down with her daughter to listen to a cut called "Darling Nikki," here's what she heard: "*I knew a girl named Nikki. I guess you could say she was a sex fiend. I met her in a hotel lobby, masturbating with a magazine.*"

"I was so angry about the songs my children and I had heard that I quickly agreed to join," Tipper wrote later about her decision to lend her time, talents, and leadership skills to the fight.

We four—Tipper, Sally, Pam, and I—soon came to be known as the "Washington Wives." This was usually meant as a putdown, a suggestion that wives of influential husbands had neither the gumption nor the right to express their own opinions. "Bored Washington housewives"—that's what singer Frank Zappa labeled us. Later he upped the ante by calling us "cultural terrorists."

We never denied that having prominent husbands helped us. Others had preceded us into this fray, among them the National Parent–Teacher Organization, but they had not gained the traction they needed to make a difference. Our husbands' names gave us political clout and helped attract media attention to the issue. We didn't think it was something to apologize for; it was something for which to be grateful.

We set up an organization called the Parents Music Resource Center (the PMRC) and opened our national office in Arlington, Virginia, in May 1985. In the weeks, months, and years that followed, we researched violence and explicit sexuality in lyrics, album covers, music videos, and concerts. We published our findings in reports and press releases. We conducted one public meeting after another to share our findings with parents and educators. We also talked to every journalist who would return our calls.

The response was overwhelming. We expected dozens to attend our public meetings, but often hundreds came. And when we wondered how we were going to attract journalists, they began to call us. Within weeks, reports or columns about our project appeared in dozens of major outlets, including *U.S. News & World Report* (David Gergen, "X-Rated Records"), *Radio and Records* (a broadcasting industry newsletter), the *Washington Post* (William Raspberry, "Filth on the Air"), and *Billboard* ("A Call for Restraint"). And this was just the beginning.

We had touched a nerve. We would not need to stir up public outrage at the violent and vulgar music flooding our music stores, airwaves, and concert stages; we would just need to channel the anger that was already there. And that's just what we did.

Public meetings were the heart and soul of our project. Parent groups would invite us to meet in schools or churches. Our script became more sophisticated over the years, but we always had the same message: Parents needed to know what degrading and destructive words and images their children were being exposed to, and they needed a strategy to help protect their children.

"When messages glamorizing suicide are delivered to an age group that is experiencing an epidemic of suicide, parents have to be concerned," I said at one meeting. "When artists tout sexual promiscuity to a generation faced with a deadly AIDS epidemic and sexually transmitted diseases, we all must be concerned."

I would talk to parents and teachers about how we perceived the messages being relayed to kids was that drug abuse was cool, casual sex was fine, rape was acceptable. And that was just the introduction. Before the main event, we would always warn our audience what was coming.

"To give you a realistic idea of what's out there," we would say, "you may see and hear some things here tonight that will shock and offend you."

That was putting it mildly.

To really educate parents, we decided to recite—word for word—the lyrics of songs from top-selling albums. "Suicide" is an abstraction. The awful reality hits you when you hear a popular singer urge an impressionable teenager to think about killing himself. When we hear "incest," we cluck our tongues, but something more visceral happens when you hear lyrics that explicitly encourage a child to consider having sex with his sister.

In the rest of this chapter, I will do for you what our little group did for parents in our meetings back then: I'll repeat the disgusting words.

If you decide you want to skip the rest of this chapter, I'll understand. But putting our fingers in our ears won't make this music go away. For the kids' sake, I hope you'll stick it out and keep reading.

One theme of punk rock, heavy metal, and (later) rap and hip-hop, we explained, was inappropriate sexual conduct by teens and sexual exploitation of girls and women.

I was only sixteen, but I guess that's no excuse. My sister was thirty-two, lovely and loose…My sister never made love to anyone else but me…She showed me where it's supposed to go…Incest is everything it's supposed to be. Prince, "Sister," *Dirty Mind* (1980).

I'm gonna force you at gunpoint to eat me alive. Judas Priest, "Eat Me Alive," *Defenders of the Faith* (1984)

Heavy metal was not the only offender. Increasingly through the 1980s, rap music took up the theme.

You see, me and my homies like to play this game…We all would line up in a single-file line and take our turns waxin' girls' behinds…Somebody say, "Hey-y-y-y-y, we want some pu-u-ussay-y-y!" 2 Live Crew, "We Want Some Pussy," *What We Are* (1986).

I do whatever I want to ya. I'll nail your ass to the sheets…I fuck like a beast. W.A.S.P., "Animal (Fuck Like a Beast)," *W.A.S.P.* (1984)

As we read these lyrics, we would show a slide of the album cover—a closeup of a man's pelvis with a circular saw blade protruding from a codpiece. The unsubtle message here was that sexual contact with this man would result in his partner's genital mutilation. Which lead us to the theme of violence, particularly against women.

I'll either break her face or take down her legs, get my ways at will. Go for the throat, never let loose, going in for the kill. Mötley Crüe, "Live Wire," *Too Fast for Love* (1981).

Not a woman, but a whore. I can just taste the hate. Well, now I'm killing you. Watch your face turn blue. Mötley Crüe, "Too Young to Fall in Love," *Shout at the Devil* (1983).

First I'll slice your tender leg off just above the thighs. Then I remove your tender arms, my passion running high. Last I will decapitate your pretty little head. A masterpiece of blood and flesh lies twitching on my bed. Why do you make me do these things? Rigor Mortis, "Dismemberment," *Rigor Mortis* (1990).

Gonna pulp you to a mess of bruises, 'cause that's what you're looking for. There's a hole where your nose used to be…What I need is an innocent life. Wanna do it in broad daylight. The Rolling Stones, "Fight," *Dirty Work* (1986).

Another theme, not surprisingly, was the glorification of drugs and alcohol.

Saturday, I feel right. I been drinking all day…I got my whiskey, I got my wine…(Saturday night) high. (Saturday night) high 'n' dry. (Saturday night) I'm high. Def Leppard, "High 'n' Dry," *High 'n' Dry* (1981).

In later years, another theme became more prominent—ethnic hatred.

Police and niggers, that's right, get outta my way…Immigrants and faggots, they make no sense to me. They come to our country and think they'll do as they please, like start some mini-Iran or spread some fuckin' disease. Guns 'n' Roses, "One in a Million," *G N' R Lies* (1988).

In the end, porn rock presents a cruel, selfish, and unloving universe in which alienation and depression are unavoidable and self-destruction is natural.

Where to hide? Suicide is the only way out…Why try? Why try? Get the gun and try it. Shoot, shoot, shoot. Ozzy Osbourne, "Suicide Solution," *Blizzard of Ozz* (1980).

John McCollum, an emotionally disturbed nineteen-year-old, shot himself in the head one night after listening throughout the day to this and other Osbourne albums. A court ruled that the First Amendment protected the singer from the parents' lawsuit.

In March 1987, four Illinois teens committed suicide by shutting themselves in a garage in an idling car. The note on the windshield quoted lines from this song:

> *I have lost the will to live…There is nothing more for me…Cannot stand this hell I feel. Emptiness is filling me to the point of agony…Death greets me warm. Now I will just say goodbye.* Metallica, "Fade to Black," *Ride the Lightning* (1984).

You had to be there to see the shock that registered on parents' faces when we read these verses. They were stunned and outraged.

"If you ask your children about this, most of them will say it's 'just music,' not something that influences their values and choices," we said. "Perhaps that's true for those who are more mature, who are mentally and emotionally balanced. But what about lonely children who lack the support of peers, parents, or other adults?"

What could parents do? We always ended our programs with practical advice. The first step we suggested was to talk to their children. We encouraged parents to find out what music they were listening to, what kinds of values it promoted, and whether those values were consistent with their own family's values. And finally, we would ask them to ask their children what kind of effect they thought the music had on them and their friends.

In 1989, Tipper and I wrote about the importance of teaching children to make wise decisions, and how it was our responsibility as parents to provide them with the tools to make those decisions. "The responsibility is not only to feed and clothe their bodies, but also to feed and nurture their spirits, their minds, their values."

Chapter Nine

A##H@LES OF THE MONTH

ᗕᔌᗏ

"TURN IT DOWN!"

That was the first reaction of most moms and dads to the "porn rock" that exploded into the American culture in the early 1980s. With its highly amplified guitar-driven chords, screaming lyrics, and fast-cut videos, this new form of music quickly captured a massive audience of young listeners.

At first few parents paid attention to the lyrics. That's one reason we started the PMRC. We wanted to encourage moms and dads to listen very, very carefully to their kids' music.

Alerting parents was the easy part, but we needed to do more. As Tipper said, "We all share the responsibility." And "we" included the recording industry that profited from porn rock.

In the first month after we started the PMRC, the Washington Wives began conversations with the Recording Industry Association of America (RIAA). This organization represented companies that sold 85 percent of the recorded music in America.

The president of the RIAA was Stan Gortikov, but unfortunately he didn't have authority to *make* member companies do anything. We believed, however, that growing public outrage might inspire him to *lead* them to do something.

In May 1985, we asked the industry to "exercise voluntary self-restraint, perhaps by developing guidelines and/or a rating system" like the one used in the movie industry. This would help parents protect their children from the explicit sex and violence and other destructive themes in some popular music.

Stan resisted. Some music was in "bad taste," he conceded, but labeling would be too difficult to administer. Still, he promised to "start to heighten awareness" of our concerns within his industry.

We didn't wait. We continued working hard to "heighten awareness" among parents across the nation, and the summer of 1985 marked one long advance by our group. Our meetings and the positive media coverage had a snowball effect; more and more parents began to speak up. So much so that in early September, we made an all-important alliance with the 6.5-million-member National PTA. Our new coalition went straight to the heart of the matter: We wanted labels on the violent and obscene recordings (or printed lyrics on album covers), consumer warning labels that would warn young people—and their parents— about what they were in for.

That's where we planted our flag, and soon the industry began a tactical retreat. By early the next August, nineteen companies had agreed to do *something,* but we needed more companies to participate and we needed a strong, clear agreement on the labels.

Then came the hearing. On September 19, the Commerce Committee of the U.S. Senate, of which Al Gore was a member, conducted a daylong hearing titled "Contents of Music and Lyrics of Records."

It was not surprising that Congress would take an interest in this issue. Pam, Sally, Tipper, and I had enlisted many friends whose husbands headed powerful committees in the House and Senate. By that fall, press coverage was hot and heavy, and lawmakers were hearing from angry constituents.

"We don't question the right of adolescents to have their own music," I said at the hearing. What troubled us, I pointed out, was "the proliferation of songs glorifying rape, sadomasochism, incest, the occult, and suicide."

Tipper explained our proposed solution. Voluntary labeling is not censorship, she explained, because it doesn't restrict anyone's access to music, suppress content, or involve government action. It is just "truth in packaging." We just wanted corporate and artistic rights to be exercised with responsibility and self-restraint.

I will never forget the tactics used by our adversaries. Some had serious practical and philosophical concerns about our proposal. In general, however, we were hit with two weak arguments. Rock-and-roll was always a bit rebellious, these critics said, and porn rock was no worse than what went before. This argument was easy to knock down; we just quoted the lyrics. The second complaint was that we were advocating censorship. Our reply: Make any records you wish; just label the hardcore stuff so teenagers and their parents will know what they are buying.

Here, once again, I must provide my own warning label: Some of our critics used the very same vulgar language against us that they used in their songs. I'll quote some of it below.

Lacking good arguments, many critics resorted to personal insults. On a good day, we were uppity "Washington Wives." On a bad day, our alleged sexual hang-ups were discussed in clinical detail, even sung about. One group called us "fucking whores," another "alcoholic idiots."

For some reason—perhaps because she was younger—Tipper was singled out for extra abuse. *Yo, Tip, what's the matter? You ain't gettin' no dick?*

One big insult was directed against Tipper and me in what I regard as a backhanded compliment: *Hustler* magazine named us "Assholes of the Month."

All our hard work paid off on November 1, 1985. That day, the PMRC, the National PTA, and the RIAA jointly announced that participating member companies would put warning labels on recordings with "explicit sex, explicit violence, or explicit substance abuse." The label would read, "Explicit Lyrics—Parental Advisory."

At last parents would have a way to check whether their children's albums—at least those from participating companies—had questionable lyrics.

Or so we thought.

On paper, we had won a big victory. It would have been easy to pat ourselves on the back, shut down our office, and get on with our lives. It's a good thing we didn't.

Exactly one year later, PMRC did an inventory. The number of explicit recordings from the twenty participating companies was down, but it was business as usual—or worse—for companies that had not signed the agreement. And some participating companies treated the labels as a joke. More than one-half of the albums with explicit lyrics did not even carry the label, and most others "featured labels that were hard to find, easily removed, incorrectly worded, misplaced, or too small to read," said our one-year report.

The industry had failed to honor the letter or the spirit of the agreement. So month after month, year after year, we kept slogging away. More research and writing. More meetings with parents. A three-hour multimedia program for schools. Handbooks. Interview after interview. *Phil Donahue. Oprah. Town Meeting. Good Morning America. Meet the Press. Nightline. Entertainment Tonight. Time. Newsweek. U.S. News & World Report. The Washington Post. USA Today. The Los Angeles Times.*

Along the way, we picked up some incredible allies, but the most important were parents themselves. Thousands of letters of support poured in to PMRC headquarters.

In December 1986, the 33,000-member American Academy of Pediatrics joined the fight. "Psycho-social factors can threaten a child's world as tragically as polio did a generation ago," the group said. "Among these are depression and suicide, homicide, substance abuse, and unintended pregnancy." And in 1987 the House of Delegates of the 290,000-member American Medical Association's endorsed voluntary labeling.

Public outrage grew, and not just because of the work of the PMRC. Most of it was spontaneous, the natural reaction of parents on first hearing the vulgar and violent lyrics.

An editorial in *The Chicago Tribune* warned what lay ahead for the industry. "If they fail to come up with a voluntary system, they will be inviting lawmakers to create a mandatory one they will like even less."

In state after state, unhappy legislators pushed bills to force the recording industry to label records. In December 1989, for instance, the Pennsylvania House voted for a thirty-five-word label that covered everything from bestiality to "morbid violence."

Facing the very real threat of having different labeling standards in different states, the recording industry finally threw in the towel—four and one-half long, painful years after the original agreement. The RIAA called it a "refinement" of the 1985 plan.

The PMRC and National PTA had won what we were asking for—a readable warning label of uniform size, placed at a uniform place on record, tape, and CD covers. Under the new agreement, the logo "Parental Advisory —Explicit Lyrics" would mark music with "explicit sex, explicit violence or explicit substance abuse."

And that was that. The PMRC had not won every battle, but we had won the war for voluntary labels. Much credit went to Jennie Devlin, Dr. Sis Levin, and Lisa Parro in the PMRC office. Pam, Sally, Tipper and I couldn't have accomplished what we did without their energy and expertise.

There was never a moment when the weary Washington Wives said, "That's that," but one-by-one the founders moved on. My involvement basically ended when Jim left public office in January 1993. Barbara Wyatt took on PMRC matters for the next few years, but the organization is now dormant.

In the early 1990s, I briefly enlisted in the war against pornography. I joined the National Coalition Against Pornography headed by Jerry Kirk and began speaking on the abuse of women and children in pornographic magazines and videos.

My presentation was much like those I had done so many times for PMRC—a lecture illustrated by slides. A handwritten note on my script for one event still makes me mad. "If this were being done to animals there would be a huge uproar in the press. I can't help but wonder where the ACLU is as women and children are being tortured."

What did PMRC and my work for the National Coalition Against Pornography really accomplish? It's a mixed bag. The most important thing we did was simply to help parents. PMRC gave mothers and fathers good information about the music and good advice on how to help protect their children from destructive lyrics.

The labeling of albums was also a good thing, but outrageous and inappropriate music is still out there, still having an impact on young people. These days, rap and hip-hop have replaced heavy metal as the main source of lyrics about violence, casual sex and abusive sex, drug use, and all the rest.

Meanwhile, I also hear that many record companies have grown lax in their standards about what constitutes "explicit sex, explicit violence or explicit substance abuse."

It seems to me that young men and women in the black and Hispanic communities are the primary targets. Rap music celebrates "gangstas," drugs, and street violence, and treats women as dehumanized objects. It's coarse, corrosive, self-destructive, pathological. I don't understand why leaders in black and Hispanic communities don't speak out more forcefully.

From a larger perspective, I believe childhood innocence—and adult modesty as well—is violated by sexually charged ads, vulgar TV sitcoms, incredibly violent movies and video games, and pornography. Ten-year-olds know how to use their parents' computers so what's to prevent them from clicking on a pornography Web site?

So many things about our modern world are better than they were when I was growing up. There are better and more opportunities for women and racial minorities. Our lives are longer, healthier, and more comfortable.

But modernity has robbed us of some of the good things. If we're honest, we will admit that we have all been desensitized to violence and inappropriate sexuality. We are no longer easily shocked. "No one blushes anymore," *Washington Post* columnist George F. Will once wrote.

How many seven-year-old girls today ask their mother what a virgin is? Too often these days, I'm afraid, they already know.

ALBUM

Mom and Pappy—Mary and Jack Garrett—raised cattle, rice, and four rambunctious children on their ranch in Brazoria County, Texas, south of Houston.

The Garrett children—Jacko, Bob, Klinka, and me—at our home near Danbury, Texas.

I always loved playing big sister to Klinka.

The Cattleman

Fort Worth, Texas, May, 1957

VOLUME XLIII - - No. 12

In May 1957. Klinka (right) and I were cover girls (along with a couple of nice Garrett family Brahman heifers) in a cattle-industry magazine.

One summer in the early 1950s, I won a trophy in the Texas Corinthian Yacht Club regatta,
along with Traylor Dunwoody (left) and Mary Stuart Masterson (right).

My mother snapped our picture at the Baker home after Jim and I returned from our very private wedding ceremony in August 1973.

Merging Jim's four sons and my two sons and daughter into one family proved difficult, but we made it! Back row: John Baker, me, Jim, and Jamie Baker. Middle row: Elizabeth Winston and Stuart Baker. Front row: Bo Winston, Doug Baker, and Will Winston.

With a bonus baby in my lap, I spent much of 1978 crisscrossing Texas in Jim's campaign for state attorney general.

A visit in the Oval Office with President Gerald R. Ford in the fall of 1976.
Left to right: Doug Baker, John Baker, me, the president, Jim, Stuart Baker, Elizabeth Winston.
Front: Will Winston, Bo Winston.

Jim's mother, Bonner Means Baker, hosted this family portrait in 1979. Standing: John Baker, Jim, Doug Baker, Will Winston, and Stuart Baker. Seated: Bo Winston, Jamie Baker, Elizabeth Winston, Mrs. Baker, and me holding Mary Bonner Baker, our bonus baby.

Sadly, President's Reagan's inscription on this lovely photograph was damaged by moisture.
It read: "Dear Susan, You know I'm wishing you the very best and still trying to get your guy home on time.
Warmest regards, Ron."

No. 1 with a bullet: targets for censure Dee Snider of Twisted Sister, Sheila E., and Rob Halford of Judas Priest

In 1985 Tipper Gore and I, along with other representatives of the Parents Music Resource Center, testified before a Senate committee on violent and vulgar lyrics in popular music.

Music

Rock Is a Four-Letter Word

A Senate committee asks: Have the lyrics gone too far?

Tipper Gore can do something you can't. She can quote the loopy lyrics of a rather recherché song by W.A.S.P.: "I got pictures of naked ladies lying on my bed/ I whiff the smell of a sweet convulsion/ Thoughts are sweating inside my head/ . . ." I start to howl in heat/ I . . ." and this next word presents a problem. How to handle propriety and make her point at the same time? Spelling is the answer. She pronounces each of the four letters, then finishes ". . . like a beast."

Few people outside of a core of heavy-metal diehards will know that Gore gets the lyrics a little askew. Not many others may even have heard of W.A.S.P. Tipper Gore, wife of Senator Albert Gore Jr., and some other well-connected women in Washington are changing all that. They have banded together as Parents Music Resource Center (P.M.R.C.) and, with the National Parent-Teacher Association, want everyone to know that rock-'n'-roll music has gone too far. "The music industry is cashing in on shock value, and parents have said. 'That's it—no further.'" says Ann Kahn, president of the NPTA. It is not only the W.A.S.P. who stand accused. It seems as though everyone is coming down on Judas Priest, Mötley Crüe, AC/DC, Twisted

Guitarist Frank Zappa, John Denver, and Dee Snider of Twisted Sister. Whatever their political effects, the hearings were certainly high on entertainment value.

Senator Ernest Hollings, a Democrat from South Carolina, announced that "the only redeeming social value" he could find in rock "is that the words are inaudible." The P.M.R.C.'s Susan Baker, wife of Treasury Secretary James Baker, evoked a "proliferation of songs glorifying rape, sado-masochism, incest, the occult and suicide by a growing number of bands." Zappa announced that "the complete list of P.M.R.C. demands reads like an instruction manual for some sinister kind of toilet-training program to housebreak all composers and performers." Nebraska Democrat J. James Exon suggested ominously that "unless the music industry cleans up its act, there might well be legislation." Singer Dee Snider showed up in tight jeans and a cut-off T shirt and fought past his nervousness to tell everyone that the band's song *Under the Blade,* allegedly a glorification of S.M., was in fact about fear of surgery. "The only sado-masochism present," he insisted.

na is being scrutinized. So is Sheena Easton, singing about her "sugar walls," and Sheila E., strutting her stuff. And Prince, going on about a girl . . . with a . . . magazine. And Mich . . . Gore's worries . . . Washington last wee . . . dred spirits appeare . . . Commerce Committ . . . putative excesses. G . . . friendly face on th . . . band. The Democ . . . nessee. The . . .

Tipper Gore and Susan Baker testify in Washington

After years of pressure from the Parents Music Resource Center, the music industry finally agreed to put warning labels on music with explicit lyrics.

By Doris Walfield

HOW 8-YEAR-OLD HELPED LAUNCH A CAMPAIGN TO CLEAN UP ROCK LYRICS

WHEN Susan Baker's eight-year-old daughter began singing a raunchy rock lyric, Susan decided to get the music industry to clean up its act.

Along with other influential women in the nation's capital, the wife of Treasury Secretary James Baker is waging war through a group she helped form — the Parents Music Resource Center (PMRC) — to get the record industry to put warning labels on rock albums with lyrics that are sexually explicit, violent or condone the use of drugs and alcohol.

And the women, who include Tipper Gore, wife of Sen. Albert Gore Jr. (D-Tenn.), want some lyrics printed on jacket covers.

"We have a whole batch of kids in our family who range in age from 19 to 30, and then we have our teens baby who just turned eight," says Mrs. Baker. "It was she who made me aware of what was going on when she started singing songs such as Madonna's *Like a Virgin* and Sheena Easton's *Sugar Walls,* which is about female arousal.

"Several of my friends began talking about the same subject which mad us to do some research on it. We found that the things we were hearing our children sing were just the tip of the iceberg. There is a big trend toward more sexually explicit and violent lyrics."

She cites as an example the lyrics to Prince's *Darling Nikki* from his hit *Purple Rain* album (over 9 million sold), which are sexually explicit for a family magazine.

Mrs. Baker, who admits daring to rock music in the Fifties when she was in high school, says there have always been some outrageous lyrics in rock, but stresses it is now more and more in the mainstream.

"What we're talking about," she says, "is far different than Elvis swinging his hips singing, 'I want you, I need you, I love you.' Now we have lyrics that advocate rape, sadomasochism, bestiality, incest, necrophilia. None the subject and it is covered."

To make the public more aware of raunchy rock lyrics, PMRC members have appeared on influential TV shows. And they are working in coalition with the 5.4 million members of the PTA who had asked the music industry for record labeling last year.

But in the five months PMRC has been in existence, it has made some headway with the recording industry. The Recording Industry of America has recognized our concerns, and many of the record companies in that association have agreed to a warning label," says Mrs. Baker. "But we have not been officially notified, and until

they do that, we can't say we have it in black and white. But we are encouraged."

In addition, the Senate Commerce Committee, which has jurisdiction over communications, recently held hearings to get the issue of record labeling out in the open. One witness was singer Frank Zappa, who said the labeling idea was the "equivalent of treating dandruff by decapitation."

Arguing Mrs. Baker says "That is ridiculous. Labeling in no way restricts artistic creativity. What it does is warn the public. And I think the public needs to be warned now that things have degenerated to such a degree of sexually explicit and violent material.

"We don't want to buy it inadvertently in the marketplace, and this is

what we are doing now. It's available to our children and we have no way of knowing it is there.

"Just like labels are put on our food and clothing because some people might be allergic to certain fabrics, I quite frankly am allergic to some of the messages certain rock stars are sending to kids."

On the other side of the fence, rock stars are giving the record companies a fit about labeling, according to Mrs. Baker, who says: "They keep talking about censorship, but what really worries them is that it is going to affect the sale of their material.

"There are some parents who may say they don't care, that such music is OK for their eight-year-old — and that is their absolute right," she says. "We are not trying to force our

sense of values on somebody else, but we are saying we do care, give us more information so we can do our jobs better."

The Washington Wives, as the PMRC is being called, are also asking that lyrics be put on the back of albums so they can be read before people buy them.

"Some of these albums may be totally inappropriate for an eight-year-old and OK for a 16-year-old," says Mrs. Baker. "So if you know what the lyrics are, you can make a better judgment."

Mrs. Baker also suggests parents write letters to their local radio and TV stations objecting if they feel offensive material is being aired, and send a copy to the Federal Communications Commission.

Mrs. Susan Baker with some of today's raunchy rock records. "What we're talking about is far different than Elvis swinging his hips singing, 'I want you, I need you, I love you.' Now we have lyrics that advocate rape," she says.

STAR OCTOBER 22, 1985 19

I applauded after Jim took his oath of office as our nation's 61ˢᵗ secretary of state.

Almost everyone in the family traveled to Washington, D.C., to join President George Bush and First Lady Barbara Bush for the 1989 White House ceremony that installed Jim as secretary of state.

Harald Bredesen looks on as Mother Teresa receives the Prince of Peace Award at a December 1989 event Jim and I hosted at Blair House in Washington, D.C.

❦

Early in Jim's tenure as secretary of state I hosted Shulamit Shamir, wife of Israeli Prime Minister Yitzhak Shamir, at a State Department luncheon.

I also hosted Suzanne Mubarak, wife of Egyptian President Hosni Mubarak.

I traveled with Jim on many of his
overseas diplomatic missions.

High-spirited Nanuli Shevardnadze,
wife of Soviet Foreign Minister
Eduard Shevardnadze, was a
wonderful hostess and friend.
Here we share a laugh with the
Georgian artist, Zurab Tsereteli.

On the very day that Jim and I visited Mongolia, Iraq invaded Kuwait.
Before we left, I tried my hand at Mongolian-style archery.

As Jim and I visited Kuwait
in the aftermath of the Persian
Gulf War, our pilot circled over
hundreds of burned-out vehicles
on the "Highway of Death"
between Kuwait and Baghdad.

In July 1991, I had the pleasure of sightseeing on the Thames with First Lady Barbara Bush and Kitty Brady, wife of Nicholas Brady, secretary of the Treasury.

Jim and I attended many state dinners while he served in the
Ronald Reagan and George H.W. Bush administrations.

After Jim and I left Washington, D.C., we hosted Eduard Shevardnadze, the former Soviet foreign minister, in Houston. Here I introduce his wife Nanuli, center, to my sister Klinka, my mother Mary, and my aunt Elizabeth Mantor.

Life away from Washington, D.C., gave Jim and me more time for fun. In March 2007, I made my first hole-in-one at Shadow Hawk Golf Club in Sugar Land, Texas.

President George W. Bush invited the whole family when he signed the Virginia Graeme Baker Pool and Spa Safety Act, named for our precious granddaughter who drowned in 2002 when suction from a faulty drain cover trapped her under water.

❧

Our 2007 family reunion at Lake Tahoe bought joy and unity to the extended Baker-Winston clan. May God continue to bless the generations of our family.

✧

*Jim and I enjoying a quiet evening with our dear friends
former president and first lady, George and Barbara Bush.*

*Cancer took my long hair,
but it couldn't take my love
of life, or my faith in God.
In fact having cancer has
expanded life for me.*

After

Chapter Ten

ISHMAEL AND ISAAC—BLOOD BROTHERS

ONE OF THE MOST PROFOUND TRIPS I TOOK WITH JIM WHEN HE WAS SECRE-
TARY OF STATE WAS TO THE MIDDLE EAST IN 1990. I HAD TRAVELED WITH HIM
TO THIS TUMULTUOUS REGION BEFORE, BUT ON THIS TRIP TO SYRIA, JORDAN,
AND ISRAEL, IN THE SPACE OF THREE DAYS I SAW DAMASCUS, THE OLDEST CON-
TINUALLY INHABITED CITY IN THE WORLD; PALMYRA AND PETRA, BOTH CEN-
TERS OF TRADE ON THE ANCIENT SILK ROAD, NOW BEAUTIFUL RUINS; MASADA,
WHERE JEWS CHOSE DEATH INSTEAD OF BONDAGE TO THE ROMANS IN THE
FIRST CENTURY A.D.; AND JERUSALEM, THE CITY OF PEACE—THE MOST RE-
VERED PIECE OF PROPERTY IN THE WORLD, AND THE MOST FOUGHT OVER.

My head was swimming and my heart was aching as the ghosts of the past
grabbed me and slammed home how unbelievably complex this part of the
world is. Thousands of years of war, with different tribes and peoples conquer-
ing, subjugating, assimilating, peacefully coexisting, building up, then tearing
down and building on top of the ruins. Old wounds passed from generation to
generation, resentments turning into vendettas; periods of tenuous peace and
cooperation, then war again.

I remember how much less complicated this Middle East situation looked from our side of the world. I felt grateful, yet a little guilty, that America is young, energetic, and unencumbered by a multilayered past trying to pull down its future. I thought both how presumptuous, and yet how appropriate, that we young upstarts should lend our help and energy to these wonderful peoples as they struggled to sort things out, to provide their children and grandchildren with a more peaceful life than they had known.

While Jim met with the leaders in each of the three countries, I traveled to nearby historic and archaeological sites. The trip started in Damascus, a very modern place, but founded more than 10,000 years ago. From Damascus, compliments of Mrs. Amal al-Sharaa, wife of Syria's foreign minister, I flew northeast to Palmyra, an oasis in the Syrian desert. It was once a trade center for ancient caravans moving along the Silk Road, east to China and west to the Mediterranean. Today scattered rows of marble columns testify to the city's lost glory.

Next I visited Petra in Jordan. Centuries ago entire buildings were carved into the red sandstone cliffs along the east side of a great north-south valley. Because it had water, this city controlled trade routes between the Gulf of Aqaba and Damascus, and between the Mediterranean and the Arabian Gulf. Today it, too, is a magnificent ruin.

Some miles away in a remote part of Israel I walked among the restored buildings at Masada. This fortified city on a small plateau above the Dead Sea was the last stronghold of the first-century Jewish revolt against Rome. Facing certain defeat after a long siege, the defenders chose mass suicide over slavery or death at the hands of the Romans.

Our trip ended in Jerusalem, a city revered by the three great monotheistic religions. For Jews, it is where David and Solomon ruled their ancient Hebrew kingdom, the capital city of the Promised Land of the Torah. For Christians, Jerusalem and surrounding lands are where Jesus triumphantly entered the city, ate the Last Supper, suffered the Passion and Crucifixion, then rose from the dead. And for Muslims, Jerusalem is where the prophet Muhammad ascended into heaven. The name means "city of peace," yet the reality is that Jerusalem has endured centuries of conflict.

The people I met on this trip, and other visits, were wonderful. In their heart of hearts, I believe, most of them want the same things we do—peace, stability, a way to make a decent living, better lives for their children and grand-children. But they are also burdened by the weight of a very difficult history.

Lebanon, Israel, the West Bank, and Jordan are the westernmost horn of the Fertile Crescent. People have lived there for millennia, drawn by the rich soil and moderate climate. Again and again over the centuries, armies have swept through the region in wars of conquest. The influences of the Assyrian, Persian, Greek, and Roman empires still mark the ruins scattered across the landscape.

After revolts in the first and second centuries, Romans expelled most Jews. Starting in the seventh century, Muslims captured the region, held it against European crusaders, and expanded their empire through southern Europe, northern Africa, and parts of Asia. Since the late nineteenth century, millions of Jews have returned, many escaping the Holocaust, some fleeing persecution in Eastern Europe and Russia, others simply affirming their Jewish identity, and still others seeking economic opportunity. The state of Israel was established in 1948.

What this all means, sadly, is that few children in this region start life with a clean slate. They begin with national, ethnic, religious, and even tribal identities that link them to unending cycles of war and peace, conquest and subjugation, migration and mass expulsion, all interrupted by fitful periods of coexistence. Old wounds, unhealed, are passed from generation to generation like sacred heirlooms. A grandfather's humiliation turns into a father's resentments, and his resentments mature into a son's armed vendettas.

The two great challenges of our time in this region are to reconcile the competing claims of Jews and Arabs for the land in the West Bank, Gaza, and the Golan Heights, and to find a way for the larger Muslim and non-Muslim worlds to get along. Too many people take sides on these issues without stopping to think. As a concerned human being, as an American, and as a Christian, I believe we can do better. My 1990 journey triggered an ardent desire to read more, listen more, and do more to understand this part of the world and its people. This chapter is written to share this passion with others and to open eyes, as mine have been opened, to the complexity of the issues.

I have no expertise as an historian or a theologian, so I know I must be very careful here. I also want this to be clear: These thoughts are mine. Readers shouldn't confuse my ideas with Jim's. I don't speak for him on the Middle East, nor does he speak for me. We share a desire for peace and reconciliation, but if you want to know what he thinks, please read his books; don't sift through this chapter looking for hidden messages.

So what is it that I have learned? First, I am a passionate follower of Jesus, but I am disturbed by the views of some of my fellow believers. (To be honest, until I became more knowledgeable about the Middle East in the 1980s, I shared many of the views that now upset me.) I simply don't recognize my Jewish and Muslim friends and acquaintances in the stereotypes and caricatured views offered by some Christian commentators. Jesus' ministry was primarily among the Jews, but He treated people as individuals, not as "them" and "us." His parable of the good Samaritan and His life-changing encounter with the woman at the well were radical in their time for the understanding and sympathy that He, a Jew, showed to people who were not Jewish. The first-century Christians certainly understood this, for they reached out to "all the world," not just people with the same language, heritage, and skin tones as their own.

I'm no Pollyanna. There are good Muslims and good Jews, but there are also misguided Muslims and Jews who do evil things, just as there are Christians in each category. I know many wonderful Muslims who are distressed by *all* the violence—not just the use of force by the Israeli Defense Forces against the West Bank and Gaza, but also violence by Palestinians against Israelis and violence by Palestinians against Palestinians.

I also know Jewish people who want peace, not conflict, with their Arab neighbors, meaning the genuine peace of negotiation and reconciliation, not the imagined peace of military victory for one side and defeat for the other. Islam has been corrupted by those who want control and power, just as Christianity and other religions have been hijacked at different times for political and military purposes. Israeli Prime Minister Yitzhak Rabin was assassinated in November 1995 by an extremist Israeli who opposed peace with the Arabs. This courageous peacemaker and his wife were valued friends, who entertained us in their home after Jim left office, and we wept when he was murdered.

So my first point is this: Accept that the situation in the Middle East is very complex, treat both Arabs and Israelis with understanding and respect, and don't assume that one side is all good and the other side is all bad. Pray as well for both sides to have God's wisdom, including the wisdom of forgiveness.

My second point naturally follows the first. We need to understand that the pervasive Arab grievance over lost land is real, not imagined. In the late nineteenth century, Jews began returning in significant numbers to what is today Israel. The first returnees purchased land, but in the late 1940s, Jews took much more land by threat and by violence, land that had been occupied for centuries by Arabs. Most displaced people were Muslims, but others were Christians whose ancestors had lived in the Holy Land since the time of Jesus.

I have tried to imagine how it would feel if Mexicans came to my family's ranch in Texas and told us to leave the houses we had built and the land we had worked for three generations because it had been theirs more than 170 years ago. I think we would be fighting mad! And without a doubt, we would put up the same resistance that the Arabs did in Palestine in the 1940s. Things might have turned out differently if the Palestinians had not resisted sharing the land with Israel in 1948 when partition was an option. But again, we have to imagine how we would feel if a world body told us we had to surrender sovereignty over our lands to people who had lived there hundreds, even thousands, of years before.

Without understanding the fact that more than 700,000 Arabs fled Israel in response to threats, property destruction, and force, we can never understand the injustice and humiliation that have shaped and motivated the Palestinian refugees and their descendants for the last six decades. Nor can we comprehend what it would mean to have our centuries-old identity and sense of place taken away. Arabs refer to what happened to them as *al-Nakba,* which means "the Catastrophe" or "the Day of Catastrophe."

Today an estimated 4.3 million Palestinians live in refugee camps in Jordan, Syria, Lebanon, the West Bank, and Gaza, where—except in Jordan—they are stateless and where, for the most part, they lack basic necessities for a decent life.

It will be difficult or impossible to reconcile the people of Israel with the Palestinian diaspora while simultaneously denying that those refugees suffered a great wrong. As mentioned before, this is a complex issue, and it is imperative that we be educated, thoughtful, and prayerful about the whole Middle East. On the other hand, it must be said that nothing—not by characterizing it as a "war of liberation" or "freedom fighting" or any-thing else—can justify the use of terror (the intentional killing or injuring of innocent civilians) to achieve a political end. Not only is terrorism prohib-ited by the Geneva Conventions; it is also counter to all human decency, and it certainly energizes those Israelis who demand retaliation and repression.

My third point—difficult though it may be—is that we should never give up hope for peace and reconciliation. I've seen what can happen when men and women of goodwill work together.

One highlight of Jim's career as secretary of state was the 1991 Madrid Peace Conference. It was jointly sponsored by the United States and the Soviet Union. Prior to this meeting, historic taboos had prevented the leaders of Israel and all of her Arab neighbors, including the Palestinians, from even sit-ting across the table from each other to negotiate peace. Jim's patient shuttle diplomacy brought them together at last. What followed from the baby steps taken at Madrid were the Oslo Accords of 1993 between Israel and Palestinian representatives (which did not bring true peace, sadly, but possibly could have) and the Jordan–Israel peace treaty of 1994 (which did).

Along these lines, I would like to talk about a good friend and peace-maker, Father Elias Chacour. I have known him for twenty years and am not surprised that the young Palestinian priest I first met is now an archbishop of the Melkite Greek Catholic Church. Arabs and Jews are "blood brothers," he says, referring to biblical history. (I'll discuss that in more detail below.) "If we don't learn to live together as brothers," he says poignantly, "we will die together as brothers."

Blood Brothers, Father Chacour's biography, gives force to his words. In 1947, Jewish soldiers forced his family to evacuate lands that had been theirs for centuries. In the years that followed, their orchard was sold to Israelis. In the early 1950s the Supreme Court of Israel granted the Chacours and other villagers the right to return to their land. Rather than permitting them to reclaim the ancient fig groves, however, the Israeli military flattened their village with artillery pieces and bulldozers.

Father Chacour, then a young man, was angry, but his family told him that as Christians, they should forswear retribution (an eye for an eye) and do as Jesus taught (love your enemies and treat them as you would wish to be treated). Elias Chacour has followed this path and dedicated his life to peace and reconciliation. At the heart of his work are the Mar Elias Educational Institutions in Ibillin, Galilee. To break down barriers, he believes, people must get to know each other. As recounted in *We Belong to the Land,* he established a kindergarten, an elementary school, a junior high school, a high school, a college and (recently) a university where Christians, Muslims, Jews, and Druze—students and faculty—work and study side by side.

Father Chacour raised funds in Europe and the United States to build and expand his schools, but they almost didn't get off the ground. The Israeli government would not give him a permit to build, even though he had the money. When he was secretary of state, Jim helped break the impasse by asking Prime Minister Yitzhak Shamir to approve permits to continue construction and operate the schools. Father Chacour's schools offer more than a *vision* of what is possible. They offer an *example*—a model that could profitably be supported by men and women of goodwill everywhere. Peace and reconciliation are possible, and we should never give up hope.

My fourth point is that some Christians, especially Christian Zionists, have been loathe to criticize Israel in its dealings with the Palestinian people. They see the founding of the modern state of Israel as a fulfillment of biblical prophecy. Looking ahead, they believe the destruction of Muslim holy places and the rebuilding of the Jewish Temple (among other things) will trigger the prophetic biblical "end time."

This belief is commonly known as dispensationalism. It was developed in the mid-1800s by Anglo–Irish evangelist John Nelson Darby and popularized in the 1990s by Tim LaHaye's and Jerry Jenkins's *Left Behind* books, which I read, but which I regard more as an entertaining *what if?* rather than as settled Christian doctrine.

A number of evangelical Protestants are dispensationalists, but most mainline Protestants, Catholics, and Orthodox Christians are not. While this doctrinal point is not a major stumbling block between believers, it has encouraged some Christians to support Israel, regardless of how harshly and unfairly it has treated Palestinians, and—at times—even to condemn the Israeli government for trying to support Palestinians. Through their political activism, Christian Zionists have also influenced U.S. policy, helping to tilt it toward Israel and away from the "honest broker" role that is most helpful in trying to achieve peace in the region.

I'm not a conspiracy theorist, and I'm certainly not challenging Christian Zionists' right to speak out. I'm just asking that they step back and think carefully about the implications of supporting one side over the other, no matter what. It takes a real leap of faith, in my opinion, to look at the messy facts on the ground—Jewish settlements on Palestinian lands, for instance—and say that this is the very thing that Jesus Christ wants. Israel may be a biblical nation, but its government is resolutely secular.

It's the theologians' job to speculate about *how* God's ultimate prophecies will be fulfilled, but even an amateur like I am can understand what the Bible says about *when*. Jesus says in the Gospel of John that only God the Father knows when the end will come.

The fulfillment of prophesy is most often a surprise. Religious leaders certainly didn't expect the Messiah to be born in a stable to a poor virgin—a girl who could have been stoned to death because she was pregnant and unmarried. Even the disciples of Jesus expected Him to be a political or military hero who would end Roman occupation and reestablish the throne of King David. Instead, He wore a crown of thorns and His earthly throne was the cross on which, as prophesied in Isaiah 53, He was despised and rejected by men and executed as a common criminal.

All of us need to be careful about ascribing our human political and foreign policy preferences to God. His prophecies will be fulfilled in their own way and in their own time. Meanwhile, our task is to try, and try again, to reflect Christ's love and His character in our own lives, especially toward those who are genuinely suffering—including both the Palestinians and the Jews.

My fifth point of concern is that we are so quick to think of Palestinians as Muslims that we often forget that many of them are Christians. Their ancestors were among the very first people to follow Jesus. Sadly, the modern-day suffering of these Christian believers has largely been overlooked by the Western Church. In effect we have abandoned tens of thousands of our Christian Arab brothers and sisters.

As in Father Chacour's story, many have had their ancestral lands stripped away and now find themselves caught in the middle in a conflict not of their making. A long tradition of peaceful coexistence between Palestinian Christians and Palestinian Muslims has been weakened. Radical Muslims are now more antagonistic toward Christian Arabs, calling them heretics and followers of what is sometimes described as a pro-Israeli "Western" religion.

Furthermore, Israeli settlers and soldiers often treat them harshly. In the West Bank even short trips are interrupted by checkpoints where delays are common and passage is at the discretion of young armed soldiers. Many roads are off limits. Longer journeys require permits that may or may not be granted. Getting to schools, hospitals, even holy religious sites grows more difficult, and in some cases impossible. Water is controlled by Israeli authorities, who are all too willing to reduce service to a Palestinian village to satisfy the needs of Jewish settlers.

All Palestinians, and particularly Palestinian Christians, have also been hurt by Israel's West Bank barrier. It has taken Palestinian land, cut off access to orchards, crops, and schools, robbed workers of jobs in Israel, and separated some Palestinian Christians from their families and friends, churches and religious sites. The disruption is especially acute in Bethlehem. Even those who believe that Israel needs the barrier for security should be sensitive to the question of where it is located and how it can be built to minimize its adverse impact on innocent Palestinians.

It should be no surprise that many Palestinian Christians, particularly the young—demoralized, tired of the constant humiliation—have given up hope, packed their bags, and moved away. Before the creation of Israel, by some estimates, Christians made up 20-to-40 percent of the Palestinian population. Today local Christians—estimated at 40,000 to 90,000—make up less than 3 percent of the West Bank total. The Palestinian Christian diaspora is ripping the heart out of a rich culture, a traditional way of life, and a deep faith that has endured for centuries. One source says more Palestinian Christians now live in Sydney, Australia, than in Jerusalem.

The emotional climax of my 1990 visit to Jerusalem came near the end of our stay. We toured Israel's Yad Vashem Holocaust Memorial History Museum and participated in a poignant ceremony to commemorate the six million European Jews murdered in World War II. This reminder of man's inhumanity to man set my tears flowing. As much as my heart ached that day—and still aches—for the wrongs done to the Jews, I also wept for Israel's unfair and oppressive treatment of the Palestinian people, which has caused much despair, resentment, anger, and violence. There are many Israeli Jews who wish this occupation would cease, and there are peace groups working toward that end.

As Father Chacour puts it, Arabs and Jews are really "blood brothers." The Old Testament story of Abraham, beginning in Genesis 12, tells why. For Jews, Abraham is the founding patriarch, the man selected by God to be the father of the Jewish people. Less well-known, perhaps, is that Abraham is also the patriarch of the Arab people.

The two lines of Abraham's descendants came through two sons, Isaac and Ishmael. Isaac was born to Abraham and his wife, Sarah, on a promise by God to give them a son even through Sarah was well past childbearing age. The Bible tells how God repeatedly blessed Abraham, Sarah, Isaac, Isaac's son Jacob (later called "Israel"), and the "children of Israel"—the "great nation" promised by God.

The other son, Ishmael, was conceived and born *before* Isaac. Despairing of not having a child of her own (and thereby displaying a lack of trust in God), Sarah sent Abraham to sleep with a servant girl, Hagar. The household quickly fell into turmoil; Hagar despised Sarah, and Sarah mistreated her. An angel of the Lord comforted Hagar, instructing her to name her son Ishmael ("God hears") and promising to "greatly multiply your descendants so they will be too many to count."

God's blessing of Isaac and his descendants is no surprise. The Old Testament, after all, is the story of the covenant between God and the Jewish people. But God also blessed Ishmael: "And as for Ishmael, I have heard you: I will surely bless him…and I will make him into a great nation." (Genesis 18:20) The Bible also says when Abraham died, "His sons Isaac and Ishmael buried him…" (Genesis 25:9)

What does this mean? It means that Jews (who descended from Isaac) and Arabs (who descended from Ishmael) truly are "blood brothers." They share a common patriarch, and most importantly for understanding God's plan, He promised to bless *both* nations.

Not just the Jews. Not just the Arabs. Both.

Can't we Christians do the same?

Chapter Eleven

FORGIVENESS

"I FORGIVE."

These are hard words for anyone to say. At times in my life I have had trouble saying them. When someone did me wrong—or worse, did injury to someone in my family—I wanted the justice of retribution, not the mercy of forgiveness. That's human nature. Yet as one who has been divorced, as a mother of eight children, four of them stepchildren, and as the wife of a high-profile government official for more than thirteen years, I have had to learn about forgiveness, both to survive and to be true to my faith.

One of the toughest experiences of our family's time in government came in the early 1980s. It was a stressful time as I was trying to cope with being a "wife of" while mothering a passel of spirited teenagers and one bonus baby. Jim was away from home fourteen hours a day. I was busy working for the homeless, keeping up with the kids' school stuff, and trying to catch them when they were doing things they shouldn't have been doing.

To complicate matters, we answered a call one night telling us a son had been arrested on a marijuana charge. This was devastating enough, but seeing the story on every major television news program, in every big newspaper, and in every newsmagazine was crushing. What the kid had done was wrong, of course, but the overkill in the media was outrageous. If his father had not been the White House chief of staff, this story would not have made the county weekly.

Reading negative stories about Jim was difficult, but that was nothing compared with reading negative stories about one of our children. The unfairness of this undid me, and I went ballistic. Families give up a great deal in public life, and it is particularly hard on children. For several days I stomped around and was so angry I could hardly breathe!

When I finally wore myself out and stopped ranting and raving, I knelt to pray for God to help me deal with my anger. In the quiet of my heart, the words of Jesus from Mark 11:25 came to me. "And when you stand praying, if you hold anything against anyone, forgive him, so that your Father in heaven may forgive you your sins."

My immediate reaction was, "But Jesus didn't know about the modern press corps when he said that!"

The terrible truth is that Jesus suffered much more than a bad press. He was betrayed by His own religious leaders and His friend Judas; He was beaten and defiled, and died a most excruciating death. Yet despite it all he said, "Father, forgive them, for they know not what they do."

In the Lord's Prayer we say, "Forgive us our trespasses as we forgive those who trespass against us." Yet how often do we think about what these words really mean?

Just after Jesus taught this prayer to his disciples (in Matthew 6:9-13), he repeated the point about forgiveness (6:14-15): "For if you forgive men when they sin against you, your heavenly Father will also forgive you. But if you do not forgive men their sins, your Father will not forgive your sins."

I'm no theologian but this sounds as if God's forgiveness of me is conditioned on my being willing to forgive others. I had a choice: either stew in my self-righteous anger or choose God's way of forgiveness. I wrestled with this but finally said, "Lord, please help me do it Your way."

I decided to try to forgive, but to be honest, it wasn't happening. So I began to pray for God to help me let go of my anger and resentment. I also prayed that journalists would become more sensitive to families and less eager to exploit the family troubles of government officials.

Slowly, my anger melted away. It didn't happen overnight, but it happened. I've often thought how easy it would have been for me to slip into real bitterness if I had struggled with this alone and not had my faith and a biblical perspective.

Failure to forgive ends up hurting the one who harbors resentment and no one else. Scientific studies show that anger, bitterness, and resentment, if not dealt with in a positive way, can make us sick, even deathly sick. There's a kind of spiritual sickness in wanting forgiveness for oneself while refusing to extend the same act of mercy to others. That is what Jesus was trying to tell us in the parable of the unforgiving servant in Matthew 18:21-34.

If we don't forgive, we are bound to relive the injury over and over again, expending our energy and crippling our emotional stability. The reality is that an unforgiving spirit binds us up; it imprisons us and keeps us from the fullness of life. If the truth be told, we are all capable of causing harm to others, and it's important not to forget this.

I'm embarrassed to admit how hard I had to struggle to forgive the press. This was a relatively small matter. How would I have responded if I had been Nelson Mandela, imprisoned for twenty-seven years because of his opposition to apartheid? We have witnessed the remarkable end to that brutal system in South Africa as a result of his willingness to forgive and to work for reconciliation, in spite of having been treated so horribly. At his inauguration as president of South Africa in May 1994, he invited his white jailer as an honored guest. President Mandela's courage and faith have literally changed the course of his nation's history.

Another good example of the power of forgiveness was offered by Pope John Paul II after a gunman wounded him in 1981. Later the pope visited his would-be assassin in prison and forgave him. "Forgiveness is above all a personal choice," he said later, "a decision of the heart to go against the natural instinct to pay back evil with evil. The measure of such a decision is the love of God who draws us to Himself in spite of our sins."

In *The Healing Power of Forgiving*, Martha Alken says that when we forgive, we further God's life among us and that our private act of the will becomes public in its effect. Nelson Mandela changed the course of his country's history because he was willing to forgive. And Pope John II, also a man of forgiveness, helped change the course of the world.

As I mentioned in the preceding chapter, Father Elias Chacour has been mightily used by God in the tinderbox of the Middle East as an instrument of peace and a facilitator of forgiveness. Jim and I have had the privilege of visiting the Mar Elias Educational Institutions and have been inspired by seeing his dream become reality. With these schools and with community centers and libraries, Father Chacour has brought Muslims, Christians, Jews, and Druze together and promoted peace and reconciliation in his small corner of the Holy Land.

Father Chacour's work is a present-day testament to the revolutionary life and message of Jesus Christ. With His teachings on forgiveness, Jesus broke the old cycle of retribution ("an eye for an eye") and opened up radical new possibilities for how we can relate to each other as individuals and as societies.

Forgiveness may be counterintuitive, but it works. Can you imagine what would happen if those of us who claim to be good Christians, instead of being so unforgiving, would take His words seriously? The world could be revolutionized overnight. The Middle East—indeed, the whole world—would be a different and better place today.

Novie Hinson, a Christian psychologist, believes the reason we don't practice forgiveness is that most people really don't know what it is. Her definition is simple: *"We forgive when we stop looking to the one who injured us to make it right."* I quote and paraphrase from her series on forgiveness taught at the National Presbyterian Church in Washington, D.C., where she listed some things that forgiveness is *not*:

1. *"Forgiveness is not forgetting.* It isn't true that if you forgive someone, you will forget the incident. Forgiveness just makes the memory a little more cloudy."

2. *"Forgiveness is not condoning.* Forgiving is saying a wrong *was* done to me. It is owning the offense, dealing with the anger, and choosing to forgive."

3. *"Forgiveness is not absolution.* Absolution washes away our sin; afterward, we are no longer guilty. As human beings, however, we don't have

power to say to one who has wronged us, "You are not guilty." Only God can do that." Even when we forgive a person who has injured us, he or she may still owe a debt to the criminal justice system or may suffer other lasting consequences.

4. "*Forgiveness is a process, not an event.*" After we have forgiven someone, the old anger still boils up occasionally, sometimes as much as ten years later. That doesn't mean we haven't forgiven; it just means we need to ask God for the grace to let go.

5. "*Forgiveness is not minimizing the truth.*" If you suffer a serious wrong, don't say, "It's okay. No big deal." It *is* a big deal, and if you don't accept the reality of the whole offense, it will come back to haunt you. *There must be a real commitment to the truth.*

   As a strong people pleaser, I tended to sugarcoat my hurts. That doesn't work. Our wounds don't go away even if we refuse to acknowledge them.

6. "*Forgiveness is not conditional; it is UNCONDITIONAL.* Don't withhold forgiveness until someone changes (or promises to) or says he or she is sorry. Jesus didn't say, Forgive us our trespasses as we forgive those who *apologize* to us." Forgiveness has nothing to do with the person who hurt me; it has everything to do with me. It is something that happens *in me.*

We also need to be able to forgive ourselves. For our insecurities and imperfections. For our mistakes. And for the careless or deliberate wrongs we have done to others. Acknowledging our own shortcomings and forgiving ourselves makes us less self-righteous, more understanding of the shortcomings of others, more compassionate. Self-forgiveness is really self-acceptance.

In Luke 6:27–38, Jesus gives us the prescription for putting forgiveness into action. He says:

> "But I tell you who hear me: Love your enemies, do good to those who hate you, bless those who curse you, pray for those who mistreat you. . . . Do to others as you would have them do to you.

> "[L]ove your enemies, do good to them . . . . Be merciful, just as your Father is merciful.

"Do not judge, and you will not be judged. Do not condemn, and you will not be condemned. Forgive, and you will be forgiven. Give, and it will be given to you."

I believe Jesus asks us to forgive others because, as one with the Father who made us, He knows that un-forgiveness is like a rampant cancer that can eat us alive. When we refuse to forgive, He knows, we permit the wrong to live in our hearts and torment us. Real healing begins in us when we can pray for, and do good to, those who have hurt us.

As His grace begins to work in our hearts, we are liberated from the bondage of anger and resentment that enslaves us to yesterday's wrongs. Then we are free to start living the abundant life that Our Lord wants for each of us.

Chapter Twelve

A GATHERING OF FRIENDS

ᑲᑐ

FORGIVENESS STILL NEEDS WORK IN MY LIFE. THAT'S PROBABLY WHY I COULDN'T RESIST DR. MACK HARNDEN'S INVITATION TO WORK WITH HIM ON A PROJECT IN THE HOLY LAND TO CELEBRATE THE 2000TH BIRTHDAY OF JESUS BY HONORING HIS TEACHINGS ABOUT LOVE AND FORGIVENESS.

I had become acquainted with Mack, a psychologist, in 1993 when he asked me to speak in Kansas City at a forgiveness conference. He made his living as a management consultant, but his heart's desire was to spread the word about the spiritual, psychological, and physical benefits of forgiveness. The more I understood his grasp of this topic, and his depth of commitment to it, the more I was drawn to be involved. When Mack asked if I would join in the Holy Land project, I signed on in spite of my resolution not to accept any more big assignments.

I believed then, as I believe now, that as the world grows smaller and smaller it doesn't have much chance of survival unless individuals, ethnic and religious groups, and nation-states grasp the principles of forgiveness and begin to put them into practice.

I quickly introduced Mack to Doug Coe to get advice about wether the Holy Land project was feasible, and if so, how to organize it. Doug is a dynamic, behind the-scenes Christian leader who collaborates with the House and Senate Committees to put on the National Prayer Breakfast held every February in Washington. He works with men and women from around the globe establishing small prayer and fellowship groups, so his perspective would be invaluable. At the time, Jim was in one of Doug's many small Bible study groups, and we treasure our relationship with him and his wife Jan.

Doug liked Mack's idea and asked Janet Hall, the wife of Tony Hall, a Democratic congressman from Ohio, to work with us. Janet and I had become very close friends through the first lady's prayer group (more about that in the next chapter), and she is one of the best organizers I know.

Mack and I were also delighted when Nassim Matar and Mark Percy joined us. Nassim was from Beirut, Lebanon, and he and Mark, the son of the former Senator Chuck Percy, had a good network of friends in the Middle East. Everyone was excited about celebrating the new millennium by honoring Jesus in the land where He lived and taught.

Answered prayer was the leitmotif throughout the planning and organization of the project. The first answer was that Jordan's King Hussein and Queen Noor agreed to sponsor our event in their country. They put us in touch with the minister of tourism, Akel Biltaji, who paved the way. Akel and Iman Rihani, an assistant in the king's office, cut through mountains of red tape to help us set up site visits, arrange border crossings, and handle logistics.

We were relying on Nassim Matar to handle the organizational details in Jordan; he speaks Arabic and still has family in Lebanon. When his wife, Maha, suffered a recurrence of cancer, however, he had to step down. The amazing Janet Hall saved the day by recruiting Brooke Flannery Anderson to go to Jordan for two months to organize the details.

But fifteen months before the event, we ran out of money. I hate to ask people for contributions, but the job fell into my nervous lap! Having already called on everyone I knew who might want to support this effort, I was in a quandary. Where would I go next? The group was praying, but the closer we came to our financial deadline, the more anxious I became. I remember sweaty palms and a pounding heart as I pleaded with God to guide us.

Then in November 1998, on our way to the Holy Land for a reconnaissance visit, Jim and I visited our friends Wafic and Rosemary Saïd at their wonderful home near London. When Jim mentioned the project, Wafic asked about the details. He and Rosemary were intrigued—so interested, in fact, that they made a large donation from their foundation that more than met our budgetary needs. This answered prayer really blew me away. The fact that the needed funds arrived without my having to make a request made me sing and dance!

Sadly, my joy didn't last long. Three months later, in February 1999, cancer claimed the life of King Hussein. Our little group was stunned, and for a while wondered if our December event would have to be cancelled. Our prayers were answered, again, when Jordan's newly installed King Abdullah and Queen Rania graciously assumed the sponsorship and played important roles in the success of our project.

For four long years, our little group prayed and planned and worked; then we prayed and planned some more. There were many complications along the way, including a major blow when our travel agent failed to deliver plane and hotel reservations. Fortunately International Traders PLC stepped in and provided the support we needed for a wonderful trip. We had to deal with many divisive issues, including issues of trust among our small group of five. The biggest problem was that Mack lived in Kansas, Janet lived in Washington, and I lived in Texas, which made it harder for us to work together to plan and organize the complex project.

All our prayers were answered in December 1999 when Jim and I boarded a plane bound for the Holy Land. Ahead lay a series of events we called "A Gathering of Friends." It would be a momentous time for our group and, we hoped, for those we encountered along the way.

The first important step for our gathering was dealing with our contrition and repentance.

As followers of Jesus we really needed to acknowledge how woefully short we, as individuals, had fallen in living the life He called us to live. Not only that, but to own up collectively to the terrible things that have been done through the centuries in His name, such as demonizing Jews and killing Muslims, Orthodox Christians, and Jews during the Crusades.

Not only have we abused those of other faiths, but we have also killed fellow Christians over points of doctrine and church politics, particularly in the first century after the Reformation.

Pope John Paul II also saw the turn of the millennium as a time to honor the teachings of Christ through contrition and repentance. During Easter season of March 2000, he asked forgiveness for the sins of the church in using violence in the service of truth, widely understood as a reference to the Crusades and the Inquisition.

"Why do we have to say these things?" one friend asked. "Haven't all religions done terrible things from time to time?" A related question, of course, is whether Christians of today need to apologize for the actions of men and women who are long dead. Do we have collective guilt for the sins of our ancestors?

These are hard questions. But I believe that we, the heirs and beneficiaries of Western history, are morally responsible for acknowledging the wrongs done by our forebears. The Book of Nehemiah says the ancient Israelites "stood in their places and confessed their sins and the wickedness of their fathers" (Nehemiah 9:2b). I think we should do the same.

More importantly, I remember these words from the Bible:

> Love your enemies, do good to those who hate you, bless those who curse you, pray for those who mistreat you...Do to others as you would have them do to you (Luke 6:27–28, 31).

Love your enemies? That goes against human nature. Yet that is what Jesus instructed people to do and what, against all temptation and opposition, we should do.

Another passage quotes Jesus telling His followers that the world, "will know that you are my disciples, if you love one another" (John 13:35).

If you love one another...

Is it any wonder the world is skeptical of the sincerity of the Christian faith? The world has witnessed Catholics and Protestants killing each other right up to modern times in Northern Ireland. It has witnessed Western Catholics and Protestants on the outs with the Orthodox believers of the East.

It has seen leaders of Christian denominations barely speaking to each other, much less cooperating to do God's work here on earth.

As our group arrived in the Holy Land, it would be a time to express sorrow for the wrongs of the past and a time to experience the joys of forgiveness and reconciliation. It would also be a time to renew our commitment to the idea that we should love our neighbors—even our enemies—as ourselves.

A Gathering of Friends assembled in Amman, Jordan, the week before Christmas. Three hundred registrants attended, 240 from the U.S. and sixty from other countries. Christians were in the majority, but many faiths were represented—Jews, Muslims, Hindus, and others. Six days of events were scheduled—a spiritual, historical, and relational banquet to celebrate the end of one millennium and the beginning of another.

Our first speaker was Thomas A. Tarrants III. As a young man in Alabama, he joined the White Knights of the Ku Klux Klan—a racist and anti-Semitic terrorist organization. After being seriously wounded in a shootout with the FBI (his partner was killed), Tommy was locked away in the Mississippi State Penitentiary. While there, he read the Bible and embraced Christianity. When he was released, he attended college, then seminary. Now he was a leading speaker and writer on racial reconciliation.

On the same program was John M. Perkins, a black sharecropper's son. As a young man, he fled Mississippi after his brother was murdered by a white law officer. John had been almost beaten to death by a KKK member. While in California, he experienced a life-changing conversion to Christianity and dedicated his life to sharing the Gospel and to racial reconciliation.

The former KKK member was now Rev. Thomas Tarrants, president of the C.S. Lewis Institute, and the angry young black man was now Rev. John Perkins, president of an institute that bore his name. Together they had written *He's My Brother*, eloquent first-person accounts of how love can transform lives and heal racial divisions.

In another event, King Hussein of Jordan was awarded (posthumously) the Prince of Peace Prize. My friend Harald Bredesen had founded the prize many years before, with the help of California philanthropists Bert and Jane Boeckmann. It had been given only twice before—once to Egyptian President Anwar Sadat in 1980, and to Mother Teresa in 1989. (In 2002, it was awarded to evangelist Billy Graham.)

My husband Jim had nominated King Hussein for the prize. As U.S. secretary of state, Jim had worked closely with the king, and they had become good friends. In his speech of tribute at the ceremony, Jim read part of the nomination letter:

> *When a deranged Jordanian mowed down nine Israeli school children, [King Hussein] didn't tell the Israelis, "Now you know what we felt when one of yours killed twenty-nine of ours." Instead, he went to each victim's home and, on his knees, poured out his grief. And the Israelis? They welcomed him with open arms, overflowing hearts.*

At another Gathering event, former members of Protestant and Catholic paramilitary units told us how they met in a Northern Ireland prison and, through faith, came to love each other. Now they worked as a team to teach the young people of Belfast—Protestant and Catholic alike—what it means to forgive your enemy and love your neighbor as yourself.

A Hindu parliamentarian from India said he had been inspired by the teachings of Jesus to work and pray with Muslim counterparts from Pakistan to bring peace to the troubled relations between their two counties. And Leah Rabin, the former first lady of Israel, spoke of her deep desire for peace and reconciliation in the Middle East.

Speaking by videotape, the president of South Korea, Kim Dae-jung, told how his faith gave him strength to endure an assassination attempt, house arrest, imprisonment, and a scheduled execution, then led him to forgive the Korean presidents who were responsible for these acts.

In 2000, President Kim won the Nobel Peace Prize for his work in promoting democracy and human rights in South Korea and in East Asia…and for working toward peace and reconciliation between South Korea and North Korea. "I have lived, and continue to live, in the belief that God is always with me," he said in his Nobel address, echoing what he told our group.

In our morning sessions, we heard from three leading authorities on forgiveness.

Lewis B. Smedes, a professor of theology and ethics at Fuller Theological

Seminary, told us that turning the other cheek is not a simple thing to do. Drawing on biblical, spiritual, and psychological principles, he outlined the four stages of forgiveness—hurt, hate, healing, and reconciliation—"a miracle that has no equal."

Using his own story as an illustration, Rev. Matthew Linn, S.J., who (with colleagues) has probably facilitated more forgiveness workshops than anyone else, led the Gathering registrants through the process of forgiveness. A young man once beat him and humiliated him in front of his students, he said. Step by step, he explained how he recovered from the trauma and forgave his attacker. His quiet, humble words inspired the audience to consider forgiveness as a path to freedom from their own emotional pain and psychological wounds.

Capping the conference was Donald W. Shriver Jr., president emeritus and professor of applied Christianity at Union Theological Seminary, who gave a scholarly—and very moving—presentation on forgiveness in politics. Forbearance from seeking revenge for past wrongs is more than a mere ideal, he said; it is good politics. One necessary step in the process is to develop empathy for our enemies. Though difficult, making friends of adversaries is possible, he said, and it is the greatest political achievement.

The final treat was a short address on December 26 by the former prime minister of Israel, Shimon Peres. He shared his perspective on the challenges of peace in his part of the world. In the question-and-answer session, he named Mahatma Gandhi as his role model in the cause of peace.

Then, unexpectedly, Peres was asked from the floor: "Would you like to meet Gandhi's grandson and great-grandson?" In fact, they were both there—Gandhi's grandson, Rajmohan Gandhi, and Rajmohan's son Devadatta. The meeting was a beautiful and richly symbolic event. On one side was Peres, a Nobel Peace Prize laureate for his work on the 1993 Oslo Accord; on the other, two descendants of one of the greatest modern proponents of nonviolence and father of Indian independence.

The Gathering challenged us to do more than just listen to speakers, however. Each day participants met in small groups to share accounts of forgiving those close to us, forgiving ourselves, and—for those who had suffered major personal losses, such as the death of a child—the need to forgive God. We also talked about the relationship between forgiveness and justice.

For some participants, these workshops offered their first practical introduction to Jesus' teachings about love and forgiveness and their first opportunity to apply those teachings to real-life problems. It was a powerful and healing experience.

In the afternoons, participants traveled in small groups to visit Mt. Nebo, where Moses first saw the Promised Land; to see the newly discovered baptismal site of Jesus on a stream east of the Jordan River; and to participate in community projects—building a playground and painting a mural at Queen Rania's center for abused children, working at Mother Teresa's hospice in Amman, painting a mural in the children's ward at the Jordan University Hospital, and cleaning, painting, and helping teachers at a school for the learning disabled in a Palestinian refugee camp.

These day trips and work projects gave most participants a deeper understanding of our spiritual roots in what is today Jordan, Israel, and the Palestinian Territories, deepened our new friendships, and made a significant contribution to the local communities.

Christmas Day began with a morning worship service from the field overlooking Bethlehem where tradition says hosts of angels announced the birth of Jesus to shepherds.

> For unto you is born this day in the city of David a Saviour, which is Christ the Lord…Glory to God in the highest, and on earth peace, good will toward men (Luke 2:11, 14).

Father Elias Chacour spoke at our festive Christmas lunch in Bethlehem and reminded us of the hope that Jesus brings, even amid the conflicts of the Middle East. In the foreword of Father Chacour's book, *Blood Brothers*, my husband wrote: "From my perspective, both as a believer and as a diplomat, I take hope and comfort from knowing that amid all the hatred, destruction and death, Father Chacour continues his patient work, softening one heart at a time."

Christmas Day, a Saturday, ended with a sunset Havdalah service, the Jewish religious ceremony that closes Shabbat (Sabbath), at the Southern Gate of Jerusalem.

For many participants, however, the most moving experience of the entire Gathering of Friends was the evening of Wednesday, December 22, when Jordanian King Abdullah II accepted the Prince of Peace Prize on behalf of his late father, King Hussein. Because it came during Ramadan, the dinner was *iftar,* the ceremonial breaking of that day's fast.

After the main ceremony, Yehuda and Esther Wachsman publicly shared the pain of having their 19-year-old son, Naschon, kidnapped by the terrorist group Hamas in 1994 and then killed in a failed rescue attempt. Afterward, Yehuda reported that he met three times with the father of one of the terrorists and reconciled with him.

As a result of his reaching out to an Arab Muslim, however, Yehuda said he was ostracized, and the Arab father was threatened by Palestinian terrorists. In addition, the Wachsmans risked public disapproval, even ridicule, by fellow Jews for attending the Gathering, an event celebrating the life and teachings of Jesus.

Also in the audience that night were Prince Albrecht zu Castell-Castell and his wife Marie Louise. Prince Albrecht, chairman of a major private German bank, has been described by one source as "a leading figure among those Germans who struggle with the remembrance" of World War II.

He stood and told the group how, just short of age seventy, he had visited Auschwitz in the 1990s and come to understand that his parents "had shown no signs of sympathy, no shock" at "the burning of synagogues, destroyed Jewish apartments, plundered businesses, and the arrest and deportation of Jews. We made ourselves guilty through unkindness, indifference, and omission," he said. (I quote here from an article about Prince Albrecht; what he said in the article is, in substance, what he told us that night.)

Princess Marie Louise also spoke, and their stories were so sincere, filled with such pain, that Yehuda and Esther Wachsman stood and embraced them. "I am now ready to visit Germany again," Esther said softly. These were the words of a Jewish woman who had left Germany for America as a child more than fifty years earlier. She had lost more than seventy relatives in the Holocaust.

"When you do," Prince Albrecht replied, "I will personally meet you at the airport, and you can stay in my home."

There it was, played out right before our eyes. This is what A Gathering of Friends was all about. This is what an answered prayer looks like.

Speaking of which, I've already mentioned how the planning of the Gathering was marked again and again by answered prayers. They strengthened my faith and my trust, which I needed. Because we would be traveling to the volatile Middle East, one of our group's most persistent prayers was for safety. And for good reason, as it turned out.

About two weeks before the event, Jordanian security forces broke up an al-Qaeda plot to bomb the Radisson Hotel in Amman, a Jordanian–Israeli border crossing, and two holy sites—Mt. Nebo and Jesus' baptismal site, *the very places we intended to visit.* Twenty-two suspects were later found guilty, and six were sentenced to death.

Was this plot aimed at A Gathering of Friends? It may have been timed to capture world headlines during the New Year's Eve millennial celebrations a few days later, with the targets being other American and Israeli tourists. We'll never know for sure. At the time, however, it made perfect sense to us that the terrorists would target our ecumenical Gathering, to kill Christians and Jews, and the Muslims who fraternized with them.

Less than two years later, of course, al-Qaeda operatives finally succeeded in capturing the world's attention by flying airplanes into the World Trade Center and the Pentagon.

Whether or not the planned Jordanian attacks were specifically aimed at the Gathering, news of the December 12 arrests frightened many participants, and about thirty canceled their reservations.

"What should we do?" I asked Jim at the time.

"I think we should go," he said. "Jordan has some of the best security forces in the world."

That helped, and I was even more relieved when the state department advised that we should be fine as long as we kept a low profile and didn't travel as a large group.

Still, concerns about security were in the back of our minds throughout the event. The *iftar* dinner, for instance, had one potentially scary moment.

It was an elegant affair, and the large formal room at the Grand Hyatt was full of dignitaries—King Abdullah, Queen Rania, the royal family, diplomats, government officials, and many others.

Suddenly we heard a persistent, but muffled, noise outside the closed doors. After the dinner, we learned that the hotel's fire alarm had gone off. It was a false alarm, but if it had sounded inside the ballroom there would have been a major panic. All of us knew about the terrorists and we would naturally have assumed an attack was underway.

What kept us safe throughout A Gathering of Friends, and especially on this night, was God's own grace, the answer to long and fervent prayers. The hotel ballroom was not a place of danger; it was a sanctuary.

For those of us at A Gathering of Friends in December 1999, the turmoil and strife of the world briefly melted away. We who organized the Gathering did so to honor Jesus Christ and His teachings at the beginning of the third millennium of His birth and in the place of His birth. But we also honored those of all faiths who practice the redeeming power of love and forgiveness. For many of us—and for me, certainly—the sands of memory will forever bear the footprints of Yehuda and Esther walking toward Albrecht and Marie Louise…to forgive and accept forgiveness…to embrace…and to part as friends.

Chapter Thirteen
FIRST LADY'S PRAYER GROUP
ৼ৵৹

"SUSAN, I'M STARTING A NEW PRAYER GROUP, AND I HOPE YOU WILL JOIN."

Holly Leachman is my friend, and I wanted to say yes, but it was a bad time to be taking on new commitments.

President George H.W. Bush had lost the November 1992 election to Bill Clinton, the young governor from Arkansas. Jim helped run the campaign for his old friend and tennis partner, President Bush, and we had all worked hard to win, but it was not to be.

Things were pretty subdued around the Baker household as Thanksgiving approached and we came to grips with the election results. On January 20, 1993, Jim would be out of government for the first time since that first exciting Reagan inauguration twelve years before. Our teenage daughter still had a year and a half in high school, so we would stay in Washington until she graduated. Nevertheless, the prospect of returning home to Houston was a welcomed one.

Holly was (and still is) an active and well-known lay Christian leader and speaker in the D.C. area. Her husband, Jerry Leachman—a recognized spiritual leader and Bible teacher himself—once played football for Bear Bryant at the University of Alabama. Today he serves as a chaplain for the Washington Redskins, and he also mentors a number of prominent Washington figures.

"This is something we really should do," Holly said. "We need to start a group to pray every day for the new first lady."

Even though I had never met Mrs. Clinton and was disappointed that I wouldn't be praying for Barbara Bush in that role, I knew Holly was right and so I signed on.

My experience taught me only too well the kind of pressures political wives face—how these pressures affect them, their husbands, and their families. It's ten times worse for the wife of the president. Everyone expects her to be perfect, and there's almost no privacy in the glaring spotlight of the White House. Everything she says and does is fodder for the press. The first lady has more official duties than anyone can appreciate, and all the while she has to support and care for her husband and her children.

In her 2003 memoir, *Living History,* Hillary credited her friend Linda Lader as the person who encouraged her and Tipper Gore to accept the invitation to a luncheon with our bipartisan twelve-member group. Linda, the founder and CEO of Renaissance Institute[5] had been meeting with us and was very supportive of our group. Several months after the inauguration, we all met at the Cedars for lunch. This lovely old estate along the Potomac serves as headquarters for the Fellowship Foundation, a nonpartisan religious organization that works with members of Congress to put on the annual National Prayer Breakfast each February.

Hillary was later quoted as saying she came to the meeting with her guard up. She apparently feared that we would hammer her on abortion and gay rights—issues on which her views differed from those of many in our group. But those issues never came up. Our mission was to pray for Hillary, not try to "get" her.

At the luncheon, each member of our group gave Hillary a special "gift" to help her in the difficult days ahead. Those gifts—intangible but very real—

---

[5] The Renaissance Institute sponsors annual Renaissance Weekends, get-togethers for leaders from government, business, religion, and the arts—nonpartisan and off-the-record.

were discernment, peace, compassion, faith, fellowship, vision, forgiveness, grace, wisdom, love, joy, and courage. We also gave the first lady a handmade scrapbook with these same themes.

The first to speak was Jan Coe, wife of Doug Coe, mentioned in the last chapter. What she said surprised us all.

"Mrs. Clinton, before I give you my gift, I need to ask for your forgiveness. Before I started praying for you, I was willing to believe the unflattering things I read about you. I was willing to believe rumors and gossip. Please forgive me for being so quick to believe the worst."

Wow! Jan's words took the prayer team by surprise, and they really convicted me.

Most of us, if we are honest, need to ask forgiveness for our judgmental attitudes toward political figures and their spouses.

"Come on!" you may be thinking. "Get real! This is America! We get to take on our public officials for breakfast, lunch, and dinner."

Yes. That's right. But what we *can* do is not necessarily the *right* thing to do. Life would be better—for us, for men and women in the public arena, and for our nation—if we were to leave our hard attitudes outside the door and treat our leaders with civility and respect.

I disagree with many of Hillary Clinton's political views. Still, praying for her regularly has given me opportunity to focus on her as a fellow human being, not just as a political figure. The process has changed me for the better, and she and I have developed a relationship because of it.

I treasure what she wrote in *Living History* about our prayer group and the friendship she and I developed:

> Each of my "prayer partners" told me she would pray for me. In addition, they presented me with a handmade book filled with messages, quotes and Scripture that they hoped would sustain me during my time in Washington. Of all the thousands of gifts I received in my eight years in the White House, few were more welcome and needed than these twelve intangible gifts…Over the coming months and years, these women faithfully prayed for and with me. I appreciated their concern and their willingness to ignore Washington's political divide to reach out to someone in need of support. I often pulled out

their little book. Susan Baker visited and wrote me, offering encouragement and empathy about events ranging from the loss of my father to the political storms surrounding Bill's Presidency.

Our prayer group continued to reach out to Hillary during what were probably her darkest hours in the White House—the aftermath of the disclosure in 1998 of President Clinton's personal indiscretions. In *Living History*, Hillary wrote, "The Dalai Lama encouraged me to be strong and not to give in to bitterness and anger. His message dovetailed with the support I was receiving from my prayer group…through the hardest days."

There were many reasons for my desire to stand by Hillary during this period, but one was the painful memories of how troubles in our family—a teenager's run-in with the law, for instance—had sometimes shown up in the newspapers. My experiences were far less dramatic, but I knew firsthand how public humiliation can hurt a family. In a small way, I understood what Hillary was going through, and my heart went out to her.

Do prayers really help in these situations? Well, they may not always change the situation in ways that are obvious to us; God answers in His own ways. But prayers certainly *do* soften the heart and strengthen the spirit of those who pray.

After loving God, Jesus said, the second greatest commandment is to love your neighbor as yourself (Matthew 22:39), and praying earnestly for a neighbor in distress—particularly one with whom you have differences—is a wonderful way to express that love.

The husbands of two women in our little prayer group, one a liberal Democrat and the other a conservative Republican, were prayer partners for years. They met at least weekly, sometimes more frequently, to petition God together. *In Congress they regularly cancelled out each other's vote,* and yet they always loved and respected each other. These two men are a beautiful example of how God would have His people behave.

Our country would be a vastly better place today if believing people prayed regularly for our president and other elected officials, federal and state, without regard to whether we voted for or against them.

It is also crucial that we give each other the right to disagree. Even when we don't see eye to eye, it is important that we treat each other with dignity and respect. When Jesus tells us to love our neighbors as ourselves, I believe He is also saying that we must treat those of other faiths, or no faith, as we wish to be treated.

Instead of respect and civility, we often treat others—especially our public officials—with scorn, mockery, and disrespect. The Bible challenges us to rid ourselves of the cynical and sarcastic spirit that motivates such behavior. "Blessed is the man who does not…sit in the seat of mockers," says Psalm 1:1. "Mockers stir up a city," says another verse, "but wise men turn away anger" (Proverbs 29:8).

One thing that might help us all is simply to remember, with gratitude, our many blessings. We who enjoy the freedoms and opportunities of America too easily forget how fortunate we are.

Rather than remembering our blessings, we too often collect our grievances, and then refuse to forgive those whom we hold responsible. This prayer from *31 Days of Praise* by Ruth Meyers has been a great help when I have struggled with the need to forgive:

> *Father, I thank You for the people in my life who seem to bring more pain than joy, for I believe You have let our paths cross for important reasons. Thank You for the good things You want to do in my life through the things that bother me (their irritating habits? their moodiness? their unloving ways? their demands? their insensitivity? their unrealistic expectations?) I'm grateful that You are with me, to meet my needs when others—even those close to me—fail to do so. I'm so glad that You are also within me, working to make me more like Jesus—more patient, more gentle, more loving—through the very things I dislike.*
>
> *Thank You too that You love these people, and that Your love is adequate to meet their deep needs and to transform their lives, however willful and unwise they may sometimes be. Thank You that You care for them deeply, and that each of them has the potential of being a vast reservoir from which You could receive eternal pleasure. And so, though I may not feel grateful, I give thanks for them by faith, trusting Your goodness, Your wisdom, Your power, and Your love for them as well as for me.*

Ruth Meyers with Warren Meyers, 31 Days of Praise: Enjoying God Anew, *Multnomah Publishers, Inc. (2002).*

And what happened to our prayer group after Hillary Clinton left the White House and moved to the Senate? Well, we stayed in business. We prayed every day for our first lady Laura Bush. When we were invited to have lunch in the White House with Laura in the fall of 2003, the president paid us a surprise visit to thank us for supporting her. One of our group, a Democrat, asked how he would like us to pray for him. President Bush paused a moment, and then asked us to pray that he would do God's will unfiltered through his pride, his ego, or what others had to say. This request gave us a glimpse into his heart during this troubled time in our nation.

As soon as Barack Obama became our president we began committing our prayers to our new first lady, Michelle Obama. We are hopeful that others across America will take the biblical admonition to pray for our leaders seriously and start supporting them with regular prayer.

Chapter Fourteen
WHY PRAY?
ᑌᐧᑎ

WHEN I MARRIED JIM BAKER THERE WAS NO WAY TO SURVIVE THE MERGER OF OUR SEVEN CHILDREN INTO ONE FAMILY WITHOUT DIVINE INTERVENTION. PUTTING ALL THESE YOUNGSTERS—SIX BOYS AND ONE GIRL—IN A THREE-BEDROOM HOUSE WAS A CHALLENGE IN ITSELF. THE FACT THAT THREE OF THESE CHILDREN WERE IN THE SEVENTH GRADE NECESSITATED MIRACLES EVERY DAY JUST TO KEEP THE ROOF ON THE HOUSE! FOUR CARPOOLS, FOUR BASEBALL TEAMS, ROUNDS OF MEALS, MOUNTAINS OF DIRTY CLOTHES, AND AN ANGRY STEPSON CONSTANTLY REMINDED ME OF MY NEED FOR GOD'S HELP. JIM USED TO TELL OUR PALS HE KNEW WHEN IT WAS TIME TO GET UP EACH MORNING BECAUSE HE WOULD HEAR THE WHAP, WHAP OF MY KNEES ON THE FLOOR!

To be honest, it was my desperation rather than any passion for prayer that kept me on my knees. I had moments of panic when I realized there was no way I could do all the things I needed to do for our family each day. While prayer had been part of my life since I was a young child, it was generally of the requesting and confessing variety. I prayed faithfully every day, but as often as not I ended up going to sleep on my knees. I was so busy asking for what I wanted and thought I needed that I don't think I had ever asked the Lord what He wanted me to do until I was well into adulthood.

As I began to understand that it is not my job to write the script of my life but to seek the Lord's will and guidance every day, my prayer life changed greatly. Today my life verse is Proverbs 3:5–6: "Trust in the LORD with all your heart, and lean not on your own understanding; In all your ways acknowledge Him, and He shall direct your paths." I need this constant reminder that *I am not in charge* and that I should bring all aspects of my life, and the lives of my loved ones, to God for guidance.

My prayer life grew stronger in the early seventies as my friend Paula Adams and I committed to pray together weekly. Joining a Bible study with small groups who prayed for each other also helped my prayer walk. The encouragement of praying with others and seeing answered prayers in their lives expanded and strengthened my faith.

Out of necessity I started asking God to show me which things on my endless to-do list were important from His perspective. It was interesting how many items lost their urgency when I had a good quiet time and prayed for discernment. Proverbs 10:17 in the Living Bible says, "Reverence for the Lord makes the days grow longer." The general understanding of this verse is that reverent people will live a long life, but when I prayed, reverence for the Lord worked to give me more hours in the day. Amazing things happened, and days did grow longer. If I didn't pray, I could count on chaos.

A concrete example of the efficacy of prayer came early in our new marriage. During my four years as a single mom, I was blessed with the help of a wonderful housekeeper. When Jim and I married she expected to come with us, but Jim had a housekeeper as well and that was not to be. I spent weeks frantically trying to find Angelita a job because my house had been sold and she would have to move out soon. Finally I got on my knees and prayed, "O Lord, please help! We love Angelita and she has nowhere to go. What can I do?"

Would you believe that within two weeks she became engaged? If only I had prayed first instead of spending countless hours trying to solve the problem by myself. This experience taught me an important lesson about anticipatory prayer.

Jim puts great stock in a slogan his father taught him, *"Prior preparation prevents poor performance."* My variation goes, *"Prior prayer prevents panic performance!"* St. Paul gave us good spiritual *and* practical advice in Philippians 4:6–7: "Do not be anxious about anything, but in everything, by prayer and petition, with thanksgiving, present your requests to God. And the peace of God, which transcends all understanding, will guard your hearts and your minds in Christ Jesus."

In early 1978 my friends taught me what it meant to "bear one another's burdens." Trying to care for a five-month-old baby, run our house with a modicum of order, plan my role in a statewide political campaign, and ride herd on some wild and woolly teenagers had almost done me in. I was having a hard time being the mom I needed to be for our children.

At the time I was on the Servants Team of my local Community Bible Study, and we met weekly to pray for the class and for one another. My friends could tell I was in dire straits, so they figuratively "adopted" our eight children. Each friend selected two Baker–Winston children, then prayed each day for God to help them deal with their difficulties. My job was to thank and praise God for each child instead of praying about the problems.

This is still one of the most wonderful gifts I have ever received. It felt as though the weight of the world had been lifted off my shoulders! My worries had stopped me from relaxing and having fun with my children. When I focused on the good things and thanked God for each child, I began to enjoy them again. This changed the attitude in my heart more than I could l have imagined.

When my sister Klinka's son, Jack, was dying some years later, Barbara Priddy, a dear friend in Washington, D.C., gave Klinka the same gift. For thirty days Barbara prayed about Jack's medical condition and about Klinka's burdens and those of her family. Klinka's only responsibility was to praise God and thank God for Jack and the other blessings in her life. "Some days," Barbara warned Klinka, "the only blessing you may remember is that you were able to get out of bed that morning, but that is enough." In Klinka's words, "The gift of Barbara's prayers at this critical time changed my life forever."

My dear friend Leilani Watt—wife of James Watt, the controversial secretary of the interior in President Reagan's first term—taught me to turn worry into positive prayer. Leilani contended that when we allow worry and anxiety to take over, they erode our trust in God. The minute a negative thought about a child (or anything else) grips our heart, we should immediately thank God for the subject of our worry, say out loud that we put that person in God's care, and visualize that person as whole and complete in the palm of God's hand. The more I practiced this discipline, the easier it was to do. Prayer is like exercise: The more we do it, the stronger we become.

Prayer partners have been vital in strengthening my spiritual life. When Jim and I were newlyweds, we lived next door to Al and Kay Ebert. Al and Jim practiced law together at Andrews Kurth, and the four of us were good friends. I don't know what I would have done without Kay. On a moment's notice I could run over and get on my knees with her over the latest crisis with our children and complicated lives. Since Jim and I returned to Houston in 1995, my friend Betsy Brown has filled that same vital role in my life.

In January 2007 Nancy Doss called on me and a small group of other women to pray regularly about Iraq. The violence and downward spiral of events there had left us in anguish, feeling helpless. This group still meets to this day. Each Monday afternoon we gather for one hour. At first we are quiet, cleansing our hearts and praying silently that the Holy Spirit will guide our prayers. Betsy Brown, my prayer partner, informs our sessions with reports on her worldwide ministry of worship and song.

Our purpose is not to rehash the past (should we be there?) or make judgments about the future (should we withdraw now or later?). We simply pray for a beneficial result from what has happened and for the well-being of those caught in the conflict—whether military or civilian, whether Iraqi or American. Our faith is in a God whose goodness and love is greater than man's inhumanity to man, a God who wants to bring order out of our chaos, good out of our evil, and peace out of our turmoil.

We believe that there is a spiritual battle going on as well as the physical one, and that this spiritual battle is the real root of the violence. We think that God has a plan to fight in the spiritual realm and that when His plan is followed, the land and the people will have a chance to be liberated and walk in freedom.

A great Biblical example of God's intervention in history is the story of

Jehoshaphat in 2 Chronicles 20. This king of Judah was told that a large army was marching toward Jerusalem. He immediately went before God, acknowledged that "we have no power to face this vast army," and pleaded for help. He also called for his people to pray and fast.

In response God said, "Do not be afraid or discouraged because of this vast army. For the battle is not yours, but God's" (2 Chronicles 20:15b). Through a prophet, God called the Judeans to take up their positions and stand firm, then to trust the Lord for deliverance. They obeyed, singing and praising God when they reached the appointed site. The confused enemies turned on each other and were defeated.

Our prayer group prays that God will reveal his plan for Iraq just as He revealed to King Jehoshaphat His plan for ancient Judah.

Our group also prays specifically for:
- the military forces of the United States, Iraq, and coalition partners and their commanders and chaplains;
- spouses and families of the soldiers;
- grieving families that have lost loved ones;
- our president, his cabinet, and his advisers;
- all members of our national government, regardless of party affiliation;
- the Iraqi government and tribal leaders;
- the Iraqi police;
- civilians caught in the middle of sectarian bloodshed;
- enemy forces;
- displaced refugees;
- nongovernmental organizations and faith-based workers;
- the media; and
- contractors and workers rebuilding the infrastructure of Iraq and Afghanistan.

Each week we are emboldened a little bit more as we realize that we really do have a role to play in this and other world conflicts, and that we *must* be faithful to the work of prayer. Praying in unity is powerful and uplifting, and God's comfort surrounds us as we cry out for help for all concerned. As I write this, Barack Obama has become our new president. We will continue to pray for him and others in our government.

Jesus taught the importance of prayer by the way he lived and by declaring, "The Son can do nothing on his own accord" (John 5:19). He constantly sought time with the Father. If Jesus needed to pray often, how much more do we need to do the same. Too often, believers forget the power of prayer. Sadly, we too often neglect this awesome privilege. Prayer *is* the real work of the believer, Oswald Chambers tells us in *My Utmost for His Highest*. Our world would be a far different place if we took this admonition seriously.

This commitment to prayer is so real and vital in my life, and yet…why do I still struggle with the discipline of prayer? Why, especially since prayer is such a restful, soul-satisfying exercise? One problem is simple busyness, but another is a reluctance to be real with God. We think we have to "pretty up" or be something we are not. Author Catherine Marshall, says, "The price of a relationship with God is a dropping of all our masks and pretense. We must come to him with stark honesty 'as we are' or not at all." That's hard. There are times when I am not happy who I am. Fear also keeps us distant from God—the fear that we must do everything right and that we aren't loved unconditionally.

At times, my prayer life just seems to dry up; I can't pray. Sometimes, in fact, I don't even want to pray. That's when my soul needs a replenishing spiritual rain, just as parched and dry land needs rain in a drought. Reading the Psalms of David aloud helps more than anything else to reestablish my communication with God. Perhaps it is David's total honesty—his willingness to be completely vulnerable before the Lord—that helps soften the hardness that can creep into my heart.

Over the years I have developed a "tool kit" to help me sustain my prayer life. The important first step is to commit to a quiet time each day. I am great with prayers on the run, but this commitment to a quiet time allows me to turn off the phone and sit down with a devotional book and a Bible for at least fifteen to thirty minutes a day.[6] Often my prayer time will run much longer, but my commitment of fifteen to thirty minutes is realistic, a promise I can keep. I try to pray early in the day, but if that doesn't work, the important thing is to catch up later.

---

[6] Some of my favorite devotionals are *My Utmost For His Highest* by Oswald Chambers, *God's Best Secrets* by Andrew Murray, *Disciplines for the Inner Life* by Bob Benson and Michael W. Benson, *31 Days of Praise* by Ruth Myers, *Jesus Calling* by Sarah Young, and *Dare To Journey: With Henri Nouwen* by Charles Ringma.

It has been very helpful to have a quiet spot in the house that I consider my prayer corner. Every time I pass this chair it calls to me if I haven't prayed.

When I first began my quiet prayer time, I would read a passage from the New Testament, because I wanted to know thoroughly what Jesus said and how He lived. If I was in a group Bible study, I would read the assigned scriptures. Then I would follow the ACTS model—adoration, confession, thanksgiving, and supplication. At first I just made my own prayers for these categories, but later I learned about praying the scriptures. Praying God's word back to Him is a very effective way of reinforcing His truth in my heart, and it is very powerful. Here are a few examples of how to pray the scriptures:

David's prayers are a wonderful guide to adoration, especially in Psalms 103–105 ("praise the Lord, O my soul") and 1 Chronicles 29 ("the glory and the majesty and the splendor"). Beautiful songs of praise from our hymnals are also good models.

For confession, I turn again to both the Old Testament—Psalm 38 ("I confess my iniquity; I am troubled by my sin"), Psalm 51 ("for I know my transgressions'") and others—and the New Testament—Romans 7 ("a slave to sin") and Romans 8 ("the mind of sinful man is death"). The key to confession, of course, is to honestly examine one's conscience on a regular basis. Betsy, my prayer partner, helps me to do that. We are accountable to each other, and our trust allows us to be vulnerable about our sins, struggles, and fears, as well as our hopes and dreams.

To pray in the spirit of thanksgiving, I like to read Psalm 100 ("enter his gates with thanksgiving") and 1 Thessalonians 5 ("give thanks in all circumstances"), then open Ruth and Warren Myers' *31 Days of Praise: Enjoying God Anew*. Finally, supplication can be guided by verses, such as Ephesians 1:17–19 (may God "give you the Spirit of wisdom") and 3:16–19 (that "he may strengthen you"), which are especially good prayers for children.

These are just a few ideas. Many wonderful books can help you find other appropriate scriptures to enrich your prayer life.

Another good tip is to look for "triggers" for prayer in everyday life. Instead of getting upset every time I read the newspaper, for instance, I have learned to pray about the people and events that need prayer. When I hear an ambulance I say a quick prayer for the injured or sick person inside. When I get really angry at someone, I ask God to bless him or her, even as I try to sort out whether I should speak up or to be silent. In a difficult situation with a family member, I've learned to back off, avoid a word fight, and silently pray for God to bless that person. That doesn't necessarily defuse the situation, but it does calm my heart and mind.

Personal suffering is also a trigger for prayer. The topic of pain and suffering is so difficult for us. The first time I read James 1:2–4, I was incredulous: "Consider it pure joy, my brothers, whenever you face trials of many kinds, because you know that the testing of your faith develops perseverance. Perseverance must finish its work so that you may be mature and complete, not lacking anything."

Consider it pure joy when you are suffering? You've got to be kidding! It took me a while to understand that the rejoicing is not about our suffering, but about knowing that God is sovereign and can bring good out of all our difficulties. If we put our trust in the Almighty we will grow more "mature and complete." The saying, "What doesn't kill you makes you stronger" is right. Among the most potent prayers are those in which we accept adversity in the name of Jesus and offer up our suffering for His purposes. These are sacrificial prayers of thanks, thanks that our God is in control even in our most painful circumstances.

One of the most excruciating times for our family came seven years ago when our seven-year-old granddaughter, Graeme Baker, drowned in a hot tub. The tragic loss of our bright and beautiful Graeme devastated us all. Humanity asks, "Why would a good God allow so much pain and suffering?" The question will be debated until the end of time. The accident was horrible and senseless, but our family doesn't blame God for it. A defect in the mechanical apparatus of the pool caused the death of our precious child.

We live in a fallen world. Illness and accidents, age and death, pain and loss—these are unavoidable. And they are compounded by human errors and by the wrong choices we all make. By giving us free will, God entrusted us to play a major role in the course of events. This is a sacred privilege and an awesome responsibility.

One of the most effective tools in my prayer kit is cultivating a thankful heart. I have a tape player in my bathroom. Listening to songs of praise and worship each morning as I get dressed helps awaken my grateful heart. I had nothing whatsoever to do with the fact that I was born. Life itself is a gift. If I get out of bed thanking the Lord for a new day, and choose to see the events of my day as opportunities, rather than inconveniences that interfere with my schedule, then I am much more open to His guidance and to having a fine day.

A good source on the importance of prayer is *The Practice of the Presence of God,* the collected wisdom of a seventeenth-century French monk known as Brother Lawrence. There is a difference in learning about God and seeking an encounter with Him, Brother Lawrence teaches. Seeking to encounter the Almighty, to make space for Him in our daily lives, is what Brother Lawrence is all about.

Among Brother Lawrence's precepts are these: To know the Lord, we must believe we have received the Spirit of God. We should pray little prayers all the time and practice visualizing Jesus. We should see Him as we make decisions at work and play, so that His presence is a reality. We should talk to Jesus and cultivate a desire to please Him. If we are serious about wanting an intimate relationship with Jesus, it's necessary to get to know him!

Living in communion with God in our busy and chaotic lives sets us free from the compulsions of our world. It gives a new perspective. We can look at our life experiences, not as endless causes for worry, but as God's way of making His presence known to us. From this perspective, life is truly prayerful and abundant.

In the last ten years I have become more acquainted with the silent practices of contemplation and meditation. I was long interested in these devotional forms, but not until I accepted the invitation of Jane Blaffer Owen to attend a retreat led by Esther de Waal did I begin to practice them. (DeWaal's book *Living With Contradiction,* an insightful examination of the Rule of St. Benedict, was a real encouragement in this direction.) Two friends, Carla Cooper and the Rev. Helen Appleberg, attended de Waal's retreat with my sister Klinka and me, and they helped demystify the process for us.

Carla or Helen would read a meditation from a devotional book or a passage from the Scriptures. Then, sitting with feet flat on the floor and open hands in our laps, we were told to relax by becoming aware of our breathing. After setting our intention to sit at the feet of the Lord and listen, we were told to clear our minds of any thoughts. When a stray thought intruded, we were to say; "Come Lord Jesus" or its Aramaic equivalent; "Maranatha." Other phrases could be used, such as "Lord have mercy on me," or just "Jesus."

At first it was almost impossible to keep my head from buzzing with thoughts—who I needed to call, what should go on the grocery list, even prayers that wanted to be voiced. After a while "the monkeys in the trees," as intruding thoughts are called, began to disappear. The most common period for a meditation is twenty minutes, but even if you can sit for only ten minutes, I hope you will try it. (A small alarm clock can be set so you aren't constantly checking the time.)

At first I kept a pad by my chair to write down the most urgent "must dos" so they wouldn't nag me. Now I don't feel the need to do that. From the beginning I was refreshed by this listening time, even when my mind was clear for only a few minutes. Today my mind stays quiet much longer, and I really miss the meditation when I don't do it.

Meditation doesn't take the place of direct prayer or studying devotional books and scripture. Usually I meditate after I have finished my regular prayers and devotional study. On a busy day, I may meditate in the afternoon. My best days, however, are when I complete all my prayers and meditation early in the morning.

Other forms of contemplation and meditation are *lectio divina* and guided meditation. In *lectio,* one slowly reads a scripture verse or a word from the Bible three or four times, then dwells on the text, seeking a deeper understanding of what the words mean to that person.

Guided meditation involves visualizing a conversation with the Lord. This description of guided meditation comes from *Shared Splendor* by Jeanie Miley.

> *After taking a few moments to 'center,' or settle down, picture yourself in a favorite place where you feel comfortable, safe, and at peace. Your favorite place may be a place in nature, a cathedral or church, or a room in your own home...When you feel centered and have the picture of your favorite imaginary place in your mind's eye, picture Jesus Christ walking toward you. Become aware of your feelings as the Prince of Peace, your Friend, walks*

toward you. Invite Him to sit down beside you. Tell Him how you feel, in your imagination, about His being there with you.

Imagine that you hear Christ telling you how much He loves you. Hear His tender voice speaking words of solace and comfort. Respond with whatever you want to tell Him.

The passage then asks you to imagine that Jesus tells you He wants to transform your relationships. "What person or persons pop into your mind? Note any feelings of anxiety or fear or anger. Tell Him exactly how you feel about that person and that relationship…"

I find these prayer exercises to be a profound way of deepening my relationship with the Lord, but studying Scripture is a necessary component.

When I began doing contemplative prayer and meditation, things started changing in my life. I had tried hard to be more patient and kind, but with little success. When I regularly practiced prayers of solitude, however, I found that patience and kindness came more easily. Another example: I am pretty laid back, except when I drive—then I am Mama Leadfoot! I tend to be very impatient with slowpokes (even though they are probably going the speed limit). Not long ago I noticed that this compulsion had gone away, and without effort on my part. This change is monumental and I am really excited about it.

The purpose of prayer should be to embrace God rather than to get answers. I believe meditation or contemplative prayer allows the Lord to get hold of me and change me in a way that enables the fruits of the Spirit to grow— love, joy, peace, patience, kindness, goodness, faithfulness, gentleness, and self-control (Galatians 5:22–23). Transformation is possible when I let go of my time and my agenda, in order to hear the still small voice of God.

Prayer is about communication with the Creator, and I think divine communication transforms us. If we think about it, deep communion with a loved one transforms us as well, so why shouldn't communing with God?

Another important kind of prayer is healing prayer. Jesus spent much of his three-year public ministry praying for those who were ill, and he instructed his followers to do the same. Through the centuries the practices of laying on hands and praying for healing all but disappeared from mainline Christian circles. This trend began reversing in the early 1900s, and in 1932 the Rev. and Mrs. John Gayner Banks founded the International Order of St. Luke the Physician, an ecumenical organization with membership throughout North America and the world.

I can't remember when I began praying for the healing of others, but it was years ago. When my church started a chapter of the Order of St. Luke, I couldn't wait to be involved. This group meets for an hour once a week to study the life of Jesus and books on healing prayer. Between Sunday services, parishioners with health needs can join us for prayer in the chapel. We ask how each person would like to be prayed for and whether he or she would like to be anointed with oil that has been blessed for this purpose.

We are taught that Jesus is the healer, and we are His agents. Our job is to be conduits for His love and compassion. It is not the strength or content of our prayers that matters; what matters is that we love our neighbors who are suffering, and that we have faith that Jesus can heal them. There is nothing exotic about this. In essence we are reaching out to others, just as we want others to reach out to us when we are in physical, mental, or spiritual pain. I know that healing prayer is suspect to many, but it is something Jesus instructed us to do. We who pray for healing believe it is one of the many ways He wants us to be His hands and feet in this world.

Chapter Fifteen

LOVE, GOD

"WE ARE SO OBSESSED WITH DOING THAT WE HAVE NO TIME AND NO IMAGINATION LEFT FOR BEING. AS A RESULT, MEN ARE VALUED NOT FOR WHAT THEY ARE BUT FOR WHAT THEY DO OR WHAT THEY HAVE—FOR THEIR USEFULNESS."

—THOMAS MERTON

The longer I live the more I understand that serving God is as much about "being" as "doing." For my first twenty-five years I worked so hard at "doing the right thing," following all the rules, that I became self-righteous and judgmental. That made me critical of those who were not on the same path. The sum of all the law and the prophets, Jesus said, is to love God with all my heart, mind, and soul, and to love my neighbor as myself. Being critical and judgmental or feeling superior is hardly a loving attitude. I was well-intentioned, but I had things backwards.

Over the years I have been troubled about how I might have reacted to Jesus and His teaching if I had been alive when He walked the earth. I have always been such a "do-things-by-the-book" person that it is not inconceivable

to me that I would have been in the crowd shouting for Jesus, the revolutionary who challenged the status quo and turned everything upside down, to be
crucified. I even have compassion for the Pharisees, those sticklers for every
jot and tittle, because in my early years I thought that strictly following the
rules *was* the way to please God. If you do everything just right, I thought, then
you will be found worthy of His love.

When I started my religious education in the 1940s the emphasis was
on the law and on being obedient, with the objective of getting to heaven. Of
course the law was necessary; it provided order as peoples began to settle in
villages and towns and live in community. Order was important, but so was
respecting other human beings and honoring the Creator and author of life.

Besides learning the rules, I also heard the usual Bible stories of the Old
Testament prophets, the New Testament saints, and the life of Jesus, including the cross and the resurrection. The main emphasis, however, was on what
sin had done to Jesus, not on His grace and mercy in forgiving all humanity
whose sins had nailed Him to the tree. As a six-year-old, I remember being
afraid I would go to hell if I died without asking forgiveness for a wrongdoing.
Fear is hardly a motivation for having a relationship with God, but this corrosive concept has been a major tool of religions trying to control behavior and
get people to "do the right thing." If we are scared of someone, a genuine love
relationship will not develop.

Being a very literal type and a people-pleaser to boot, I took this message of
strict obedience to heart. I had many friends, so I couldn't have been too much
of a stick-in-the-mud, but if the sign said, "DON'T WALK ON THE GRASS,"
you can bet I didn't walk on the grass! It took my life's falling apart in my late
twenties for me to question this legalistic approach to faith and God.

I had tried every way I knew to do what was right, yet my world had come
crashing down around me. In my pain and sadness, I did some unacceptable
and hurtful things that would have made me faint just a few years before. In
my desolate and confused situation, my fall from grace was big. Because faith
had played such a major role in my life, I accepted that I had to seriously ex-
plore whether it was valid. And if so, where had I gone so wrong to end up in
this painful place?

I have written in Chapter Three about my faith journey. By the time I was thirty-five, it was a new season for me. In the words of Psalm 103, I was redeemed from the pit. My fear of never marrying again proved groundless. My attitude of seeing the Almighty as the Good Taskmaster in the Sky was replaced by an ever-growing awareness of His love and infinite mercies. My backward idea—"If I keep all the rules, life will go well with me"—was being replaced with gratitude for a loving God who would be with me always, regardless of the circumstances in my life, good or bad.

When I was a child and young woman, faith in God—or rather what I thought of as my faith—was a given. Even though it meant a lot to me, my faith was shallow. In essence I had assumed my parents' faith as my own. When my expectations of God didn't match up with the events of my adult life, I had to start back at square one. I have heard the expression, "God has no grandchildren." Now I get it.

Being so confused as an adult, after having spent a childhood that was so certain about matters of faith, was very uncomfortable. Things that had been so clear, so black and white, now challenged me. I wanted to believe, but honestly at that point "there was no there there." I was looking for simplicity and certainty, but they didn't exist for me any more. One of the first Scriptures I learned at Teddy Hurd's home Bible Study was Romans 10:17. It was an anchor I desperately needed: "Consequently, faith comes from hearing the message, and the message is heard through the word of Christ."

I had often read the Bible, but much of it was Greek to me. When I started going to Bible Study Fellowship and later Community Bible Study, which gave the background and history of the words of the Old and the New Testaments, things started to make sense. I mentioned in Chapter Three what a relief it was to learn that our salvation is a gift from God when we confess our sins and choose to believe and trust in Him instead of ourselves or something else.

If we are in a love relationship with someone, our desire is to please that person. Out of love and gratitude for what God has done for us comes a genuine desire to please Him. Knowing that God loves us unconditionally brings joy and transformation.

Before I understood this, *righteousness* was a demanding and terrible word. It seemed to mean that we had to be perfect and never sin, which is impossible. Nobody can do it, not even the Apostle Paul: "For what I do is not the good I want to do; no, the evil I do not want to do—this I keep on doing… What a wretched man I am!" (Romans 7:19, 24a) Learning that righteousness is not about performance, but about trusting in God and having a relationship with Him, was life-changing good news for me.

A theme, which some call the *scarlet thread,* begins in the book of Genesis and continues through the New Testament. It is God's promise that He will make final and absolute provision for the problem of sin that separates us from Him.

The Old Testament sacrificial system pointed toward the time when Jesus would make the sacrifice as the ultimate Passover lamb—by giving his life on the cross out of love for us.

Example after example illustrates how God wishes to have a real relationship with all people. He expresses His loving heart for us through the analogy of marriage, the most intimate and cherished of all relationships. (See Isaiah 54:6; Ezekiel 16; and Song of Songs 2.) These are word pictures to help us understand how God offers us intimacy, forgiveness, refuge, and love, even to the point of his own death.

The Old Testament also says God's love is even stronger than the love of earthly parents for their own children. "Though my father and mother forsake me, the LORD will receive me" (Psalm 27:10). "'Can a mother forget the baby at her breast and have no compassion on the child she has borne? Though she may forget, I will not forget you! See, I have engraved you on the palms of my hand…'" (Isaiah 49:15–16a).

Our Creator is like a caring spouse and parent who does not want his or her loved ones to self-destruct. God's love is not an indulgent love. It calls us to be our best. It calls us to a lifelong process of serving Him and our fellow man in love. Many Christian scholars say the Bible progressively unfolds the nature of a loving God, who is most perfectly seen in Jesus Christ.

Putting my trust in God was a hard concept for me. Growing up in the country, we were taught to be independent and self-sufficient. The positive side of self-reliance is that you learn to do a job well without depending on others: you accept responsibility and you do your job without expecting others to finish it for you. For me, the negative side is that I needed to be in charge of all aspects of my life. Given all the broken china in my life, my old "do-it-myself" attitude is ludicrous today. But when I was young I took the adage, "God helps those who help themselves," as a call to be in control. Too bad I wasn't as familiar with the wisdom of the Scripture: "Trust in the LORD with all your heart, and lean not on your own understanding; in all your ways acknowledge Him, and He shall direct your paths" (Proverbs 3:5–6).

As a girl and young woman, I was pretty good at getting my own way. My methods were pleasant and diplomatic rather than confrontational, but manipulation disguised as something else is still manipulation! This attitude carried over in my early married life as a wife and mother. I thought my job involved getting my husband and children to do what I thought was best for them. Again, I was well-meaning but misguided.

Catherine Marshall's *Beyond Our Selves* is a wonderful, practical book on faith that helped me understand what trusting God is all about. Her chapter on relinquishment has been life-changing for me. To relinquish, or let go, of our will in favor of God's will is paramount if we want to follow God's path for our lives. Even Jesus came to do the Father's will, not his own, but this is such a hard thing to put into practice. First, it means I must choose to be obedient; second, I must also spend time in prayer, listening for that "still small voice" that helps guide and direct.

I have always loved trying to figure things out and coming up with a plan. Trusting can be a struggle because it often means letting go of the plan I thought would work best. Learning to be quiet and ask the Lord's guidance before I make a plan is better than embarking on a hasty plan, and then having to ditch it because it is unworkable. One of the blessings of being a septuagenarian is that I now save energy by asking God's advice *before* I tear out with a plan of my own!

To be truthful, trusting God is a liberating concept; my old backward idea of control is exhausting and robs me of peace. As hard as I try to hold on and control things, deep down I know it is impossible. If it weren't so embarrassing I could write a whole chapter of examples of how I think I have let go and trusted God with a situation, only to snatch it back again. If only I could remember that my job is to love my family and friends, pray for them, and respect their rights, responsibilities, and boundaries. Family harmony might not be so elusive if we all practiced this principle.

To remind me not to try so hard to play God, I keep this sign on my fridge:

—DEAR CHILD, DO NOT FEEL COMPLETELY, TOTALLY, IRREVOCABLY RESPONSIBLE FOR EVERYTHING. THAT'S MY JOB!
LOVE, GOD

When I look back over my life, I am amazed at how often this theme of playing God pops up. The Scriptures show it has always been like that. In the creation story, for example, Adam and Eve's good relationship with God ran into trouble when they were seduced by the idea that if they ate the forbidden fruit, they would become "like God."

It is cold comfort to know that my tendency to think I can be in charge goes all the way back to Adam and Eve. When they were caught, Adam and Eve first blamed the serpent, then each other, then God. Their choice to trust the serpent instead of God resulted in their expulsion from Paradise. But God's tender act of sewing the skins to cover their nakedness, of which they were now ashamed, demonstrated His love and caring despite their disobedience. And you don't have to take a literal view of the creation story to see the truth in it.

In *Stories Jesus Still Tells,* John Claypool says our earliest ancestors believed the serpent's version of divine reality. They believed God was not essentially good and loving, but instead a vicious exploiter who was to be feared. Primitive religions demanded blood. In the Greek myths, the gods regarded humanity with contempt and rained down wrath from Mount Olympus. Fear was the order of the day, and retribution seemed to be the defining characteristic of the deities.

Jesus' big challenge was to show us the reality of God's love and how the Father desires to share his joy with us. He caused a huge scandal by teaching and living in a way that showed God's love to all people. The Pharisees believed that the poor and sick suffered because they were unrighteous, and that men and women who were better off had wealth and health as a reward for being good and deserving. Jesus upset the whole social order by showing respect and love to outcasts and sinners, and was killed for it. His parables make clear that He came for the lost, which is good news because, to be honest, I think we are all lost. "All have sinned and fall short of the glory of God," Paul wrote (Romans 3:23).

Jesus told a parable about a king who invited disreputable street people—who represent us—to a rich wedding. "Go to the street corners and invite to the banquet anyone you find," he told his servants (Matthew 22:9–10). On the same theme, Luke 15 tells parables of the lost sheep, the lost coin, and the lost son. When the shepherd finds the lost sheep—us again—"he joyfully puts it on his shoulders and goes home" (15:5–6a). The woman who finds her lost coin—which represents sinners, us—"calls her friends and neighbors together and says, 'Rejoice with me…'" (15:9)

You would think that after 2000 years we would finally get the message that Jesus tried so hard to make us understand, even through His sacrificial death: We are loved; we are loved beyond how we love anything, even our own children; and this love is *not* based on our performance. It is based on our God's divine nature, which is love, and on His desire to share that love and joy with us.

Instead of accepting this love and passing it on, it seems that we keep playing the shame-and-blame games that have poisoned lives since the beginning of time, games of moral superiority: "I'm right, you're wrong"; "I win, you lose." It was humbling to realize some years ago how much I needed to be right and how defensive I became when challenged.

This realization has made a big difference in my attitude and how I deal with relationships. Our egocentric selves resist taking Jesus at His word that the selfish ego must die if we are to live abundant lives. If we can accept that those at the bottom, the losers, are really the winners when they acknowledge that they need God's help, then we are beginning to understand the Kingdom of God. "For whoever wants to save his life will lose it, but whoever loses his life for me will find it" (Matthew 16:25).

I like the Rev. Pittman McGehee's interpretation of this verse. Once dean of Christ Church Cathedral in downtown Houston, Pittman is now a Jungian analyst. He says God created each of us with special gifts, and our job is to discern our essence, who we are meant to be, and give that away to the world.

Jesus' last directive to his followers was to spread the good news to the ends of the earth. I remember having a Eureka! moment when I realized He didn't tell us to stamp out evil. Life under the Roman occupation was rife with corruption, brutality, and decadence, but Jesus didn't address the social, political, or moral ills head-on. Instead, He kept bringing us back to the individual and to our heart attitude, challenging us to deal with the evil within ourselves. His goal was to change the hearts of His followers. "First take the plank out of your own eye, and then you will see clearly to remove the speck from your brother's eye" (Matthew 7:5).

Jesus knew that living joyful, trusting lives in service to others would counter evil much more effectively than waging a personal or political crusade. Too often we, believers, seem to be more interested in the numbers of our converts than in caring about them individually. We say, "Jesus is the way," but then we don't reflect our beliefs in the way we live. Some surveys say Christians are hard to distinguish from the population-at-large on marital infidelity, alcoholism, gambling, and other destructive behaviors. Gallup reported that only 44 percent of Christians said God has called them to be involved in the lives of the poor and suffering, which is mind-boggling. *All* Christians are called to love their neighbor as themselves and to care in a material way for "the least of these." It is important that the Gospel I believe in is validated by the way I live.

As the Rev. Dr. Russell Levenson, our pastor at St. Martin's Episcopal Church in Houston, has said, the Easter story is about the horrors of our humanity and about how God wants to redeem us. Through the passion and death of Jesus, we see that God is not on the periphery of our sin and suffering, but that He actually takes sin and suffering on Himself. Instead of calling the judgment of God down on those who were killing Him, Jesus called for them to be forgiven, just as He calls for us to be forgiven when we fail to live according to His teachings. This is the good news. Our failures are so much smaller than God's goodness and love. And our God is a God of second, third, fourth, and fifth chances without end or limit.

Mike Deaver's life shows God's redeeming power. In Chapter One, I spoke of this close friend who was deputy chief of staff in the first term of the Reagan White House and a trusted confidante of Nancy and Ronald Reagan. Mike had an amazing career in government and in public relations, then pride and addiction almost derailed his life. But as Jim said in his eulogy, Mike sought God's help and "pride gave way to humility…addiction to sobriety…bitterness to peace of mind…and a preoccupation with self to a selfless caring for others."

Mike used his energy and many talents to help start Clean and Sober

Streets, a substance abuse and treatment program in Washington, D.C. His caring and guidance helped redeem the lives of many friends and hundreds of people who had been living on the street.

When he died, Mike was vice chairman of Edelman, the world's largest independent public relations company, but as the Rev. Spencer Rice said, "Mike saw the promise of God in everyone he met."

At Mike's memorial service, Henry Pierce told how he first entered the shelter at six-thirty one Friday morning fifteen years earlier, ready to take his own life. He had lost everything, including hope. Mike Deaver was there to give him a cup of coffee, treat him with dignity, and help restore his will to live. Now Henry, once a heroin abuser, is executive director of Clean and Sober Streets.

The older I become, the more I believe that "seeing the promise of God in everyone we meet" is one of the best ways to love our neighbor and to honor God. Choosing to see the promise of God in people does away with my judgmental, critical attitudes and triggers a positive response to be supportive. It derails the superiority complex, the backwards thinking that comes to one who is sure he or she has all the answers. It levels the playing field in a way that I believe Jesus did when he palled around with publicans and sinners. God loves each of us, regardless of our situation in life and regardless of how we feel about Him.

It's hard for me to believe that it has been more than forty years since my immature faith collapsed, and I struggled with the questions like "Who is God, and what does He expect of me?" The most difficult part of the journey has been, and still is, letting go of my will in favor of God's will.

Our happy family reunion in Tahoe—the one I described in Chapter One—defied the odds. It would never have been possible without much grace, and many hard "letting go" lessons for all of us. My journey has been strenuous, but I am so grateful to have been liberated from earnest misconceptions and the bondage that came from believing my relationship with God was based on performance. We glimpse the Kingdom of God when we know it is not about "earning and deserving" but about "believing and receiving." As I move from law to grace, performance behavior to relationship, bondage to freedom, control and manipulation to release, fear to courage (sort of !), and conditional love to agape love, I have a peace that amazes me even though I am far from the mark. I have certainly *not* arrived, but at least I know where I want to go. And Jesus is the one who is showing me the way.

I am compelled to follow Him because love is irresistible. I know I'm loved as I am, "warts, wrinkles, hang-ups, and all." And the more I know this, the more capacity I have for loving others. This poem, a variation of a poem by Carol Wimmer, sums up my journey in a beautiful way:

When I say, "I am a Christian"
I'm not shouting, "I'm clean livin'!"
I'm whispering, "I was lost,
Now I'm found and forgiven."

When I say, "I am a Christian"
I don't speak of this with pride.
I'm confessing that I stumble
And need Christ to be my guide.

When I say, "I am a Christian"
I'm not trying to be strong.
I'm professing that I'm weak
And need His strength to carry on.

When I say, "I am a Christian"
I'm not bragging of success.
I'm admitting I have failed
And need God to clean up my mess.

When I say, "I am a Christian"
I'm not claiming to be perfect.
My flaws are far too visible,
But God believes I am worth it.

When I say, "I am a Christian"
I still feel the sting of pain.

I have my share of heartaches,
So I call upon His name.

When I say, "I am a Christian"
I'm not holier than thou,
I'm just a simple sinner
Who received God's good grace, somehow![7]

When I tearfully decided forty years ago to "let go and let God" be in charge, I thought my life was over. When I think of the adventures I have had since then I am truly astounded! In the book of Joel, we read that the Lord "will restore to you the years that the locust hath eaten." I am passing on my life's experiences and lessons because it is through them that I have learned how extravagantly God loves each one of us, and how profoundly He can restore our lives. When we allow Him into our hearts, He transforms us in ways we never could have imagined, and we become the authentic, loving beings we were created to be. When God's love is alive in us He works not just for us, but through us.

We all have our plans, but God has a better one. Pass it on!

---

[7] This is the widely circulated Internet version of an original (and somewhat different) poem by Carol Wimmer.

AFTERWORD

THE SUMMER SURPRISE

THE FIRST HALF OF 2009 HAD BEEN REALLY BUSY, AND JIM AND I WERE EXCITED ABOUT GETTING AWAY FOR SOME GOOD REST AT OUR 100-YEAR-OLD CABIN IN WYOMING. FOR THE LAST TWENTY YEARS, THE VAST OPEN SPACE, BEAUTY, AND SOLITUDE OF THIS REMOTE LOCATION IN THE WIND RIVER MOUNTAINS HAVE HELPED RESTORE OUR SOULS AND BODIES. AFTER WYOMING, WE PLANNED TO JOIN SEVERAL OTHER COUPLES FOR AN AUGUST CAPE BUFFALO HUNT IN TANZANIA, FOLLOWED BY A PHOTOGRAPHIC SAFARI IN BOTSWANA. WE COULDN'T WAIT!

As I was doing my last-minute packing the day before we were to leave for Wyoming, my gynecologist telephoned. During a routine yearly exam, I had felt some tenderness when she examined the pelvic area, and she had prescribed an ultrasound to check it out. Now she was calling to let me know that the sonogram of my ovaries looked suspicious. She advised me to have further tests at M.D. Anderson, the renowned cancer center in Houston.

This was unwelcome news because the tests would delay our trip to the mountains, but I wasn't unduly worried; I had experienced ovarian cysts in the past. For the previous three years, I had had the CA-125 blood test for ovarian cancer and had never had an abnormal result. Nor had I experienced any of the symptoms often associated with ovarian cancer: abdominal pain or discomfort, back pain, bloating, urinary urgency, constipation, vaginal bleeding, weight loss, or fatigue.[8]

My email to the children on July 10 read as follows:

Dear Ones,

Well, it has been quite a day—10:30 to 8:30! Must say that I now understand why M.D. Anderson gets such rave reviews—wonderful, helpful people, a great atmosphere, and they are almost painless! I had some tests that show that the growths in the troubling sonograms are not cysts, and doctors won't know until they are removed if they are benign.

Results of today's tests will be available on Monday or Tuesday, so we will know more then. I still have another test or two to go next week. There are good signs along with the troubling ovaries: All the blood work is great, and I have none of the physical symptoms associated with ovarian cancer.

The doctor recommends surgery, and of course that is the smart thing to do. It may happen week after next. This means that we will not be going to Wyoming, but I'm still hopeful about Africa. The prayer request now is that the surgery can be done by laparoscopy, which offers a much quicker recovery than regular surgery. Thankfully I feel strong as ever.

Your prayers have kept me floating. I have had a really nice day in spite of the tests, and feel positive that things will be well. Your Dad was a wonderful help, and we are planning on a really nice, restful weekend. I'm sure you will have a million questions, but understand that I won't know how to answer them yet. So please be patient and just keep praying. I promise to keep you as informed as I am.

When I was checking my messages tonight I heard from the publisher at Bright Sky Press that she liked my manuscript and wants to talk to me about proceeding. Yippee! This was a very happy note on which to end the day. I feel

---

[8] My gynecologist had informed me that the CA-125 blood test was not reliable, and now I see why it is not a good screening test for ovarian cancer. Although it is the best test we have, the count of the marker protein is elevated in only 50 percent of cases of early ovarian cancer, which means that normal counts can provide a false sense of security. False positives are also a problem. The CA-125 count is elevated in many benign conditions such as fibroids, as well as lung and liver disease, often leading to unnecessary testing, surgery, and anxiety.

so blessed to be in a place with such good medical care and to have such a car-
ing family to support me. Getting the book published will be icing on the cake.
  I love each one of you dearly,
  Mom, Suzoo, etc.

One week later I underwent a complete hysterectomy, in which my uterus, ovaries, fallopian tubes, and cervix were removed. In addition, the doctors removed my omentum (the fatty lining that hangs over the intestines) because there were several suspicious growths on it. While not cancerous at the time of surgery, these spots had the potential to develop into a malignancy. My ovaries, which should have been the size of almonds because I was twenty years past menopause, were the size of oranges. The surgeons were encouraged because the initial pathology report looked okay, and there was no fluid in the ovaries or the stomach cavity. (Fluids usually indicate cancer.) When the full pathology reports came in Friday morning, however, the news was scary: I had low-grade serous ovarian cancer in both ovaries. Serous tumors are the most common type of epithelial ovarian cancer, which arises from the cells on the surface of the ovary. The good news was that the cancer didn't appear to have spread outside the ovaries. It was also good news, I learned later, that my surgeons were gynecologic oncologists. *A Guide to Survivorship for Women with Ovarian Cancer* (Johns Hopkins University Press) says that specialist surgeons achieve better outcomes with ovarian cancer than do general surgeons.

To say I was surprised at this diagnosis is a real understatement. Exercise and a healthy diet are givens at our house. There is no history of cancer in my immediate family, and I have been healthy as a horse for more than seven decades. My other risk factors were also low. Ovarian cancer is less common in women who had a first pregnancy at an early age and were of older age for a final pregnancy; my first child was born when I was twenty-two and my fourth when I was near forty. The risk of ovarian cancer is also lower in women who have had a tubal ligation, which I had after my last child was born. Breast feeding also supposedly lowers the risk, as does use of oral contraceptives for ten years or more, and I fit those bills as well.

The shock of being told I had cancer knocked me for a loop. Until then, I had not fretted about the possibility of cancer, because I just don't believe in worrying about things that might never happen. (When you have eight children, that approach is necessary for survival!) So that Friday morning I was overwhelmed by the diagnosis and the powerful emotions it triggered. I wanted time alone to sort this out, so I encouraged Jim to fly on to Wyoming with a fishing buddy. He was reluctant, but finally agreed.

The week that Jim was gone was a very important one for me because it gave me time to work through my anxiety, disappointment, and anger. My body had failed me. And after I had taken such very good care of it! I loved those wonderful ovaries; they had produced the eggs that gave me four of my fabulous children. Now they were diseased and threatened my life. I cried, I moped, I was sad and dismayed. Most of all, I was scared. I also grieved that our great plans for the summer would go unfulfilled and that instead I would feel awful from the six chemotherapy sessions prescribed to catch any cancer cells that might still be present.

Looking death in the eye was daunting, and I was especially anguished by this thought: What if the cancer comes back for me as it has for so many of my friends? Thinking about being bald was also traumatic, especially since at seventy-one I believed my hair was one of the few good physical assets I had left. Hair should not be a major concern, of course, but I have had long hair for most of my life. It is definitely part of my persona. I chastised myself for feeling grumpy that I wouldn't leave this world with all of my body parts. A few months later I realize that feeling grumpy about my hair loss and the removal of body parts isn't silly—these are real emotional issues that need recognition and acceptance.

Being alone was helpful. It was such a relief not to have to show a stiff upper lip for Jim's benefit, not to pretend I was okay when I actually felt like a barnyard expletive. I was delighted, of course, that he called several times a day to see how I was doing, but I worried about how hard the diagnosis had hit him. He had experienced his first wife's battle with breast cancer and her death when she was only thirty-eight. Seven of our eight children had lost a parent when they were young, so I knew this was really tough for them as well.

I read Scripture and my devotionals and tried to pray, but words just wouldn't come. A prayer, given to me by a dear pal before my trouble, saved the day. It goes, "I love you Jesus, I praise you, I thank you, and I trust you." I focused on "I trust you" and used that as my mantra when waves of sadness and anxiety overwhelmed me. I just kept praying to really trust God and not be afraid for what the future would bring.

By the time Jim returned home, I had run the gamut of feelings and fears, and my heart was at peace. I had looked at the worst and made the choice to trust God with my body and my future. Years ago, I had given my will and my heart to God; now I realized I needed to give Him my body as well. I knew that He would give me the grace to get through this new season and all that goes along with it.

I don't believe for one minute that God zapped me with cancer. Of course He allowed it into my fallen human body, but I don't believe it was to teach me a lesson. I do know in my deepest being that He will use this experience for good if I am willing to cooperate with His grace, and that is my plan.

Initially Jim considered canceling the trip to Africa, but our friends had signed up because of us and bailing out wasn't really an option. I was delighted when he invited our two daughters to accompany him in my place, one on the hunting safari and the other on the photographic safari. That gave me joy and helped ease the sting of missing our much-anticipated trip.

My first chemo treatment took place less than three weeks after my operation. If I had it to do over again, I wouldn't have started the chemo so soon. The doctors had told me that I could wait to begin the treatment because it was a low-grade cancer, but I really wanted to get on with the program. All went well during the six-hour infusion of carboplatin (which binds with the DNA of cancer cells to prevent them from dividing and reproducing) and paclitaxel (a plant alkaloid that attacks the cancer cell's apparatus for dividing and replicating itself). Thankfully, the next twenty-four hours were uneventful as well. Then the Mack truck hit. For the next four to five days, I hardly had the energy to lift my head off the pillow. Fortunately this therapy has been perfected over the last twenty years, and doctors give Benadryl, dexamethasone, and ondansetron (Zofran) before the cancer drugs to mitigate side effects of nausea and diarrhea.

Dexamethasone, a steroid, helps prepare the body to receive the drugs instead of fighting them. Benadryl, an antihistamine, helps prevent an adverse drug reaction, and Zofran is a great antinausea med. I felt woozy but was never actively ill, and the antinausea pills that I took for the next three days helped me sleep. The hardest thing was making myself eat three meals a day because the thought of food was revolting. I also made myself take several walks a day to strengthen my body and keep the circulation going. Most difficult of all, however, I felt like I was at the bottom of a deep well, unable to think clearly or make decisions. I had no desire to do anything but pull the covers over my head.

Research by the National Institutes of Health shows that acupuncture helps deal with the side effects of chemotherapy. M.D. Anderson has incorporated an acupuncture program into its wide array of support systems. After five days I felt strong enough to see a Chinese doctor I had consulted before. She uses a technique similar to acupuncture in that it stimulates the body's energy pathways, boosting the immune system and strengthening vital organs. I don't know the "ins and outs" of how this healing system works, but it has made a big difference in how I feel, and I will continue to use it. The effects of my second chemo treatment were less severe, and I believe it was because I had been seeing the Chinese doctor regularly. I am delighted that many Western doctors now see a place in our culture for the wisdom of Eastern medicine and a holistic approach. Our health-care system would benefit on many levels from collaboration with the preventive, noninvasive Eastern approach.

After Jim left on the trip, my angel sister Klinka came to nurse me. She cheered my spirits and made food taste palatable again. I improved so much that I was strong enough to attend a memorial service on the first anniversary of the airplane crash that had taken the lives of Tommy Jacomini, his wife Susie, and their two children, Thomas and Vivi.

Tommy was one of my youngest son's best pals from childhood, and I had gone to high school and college with his parents, who are still dear friends. It had been a year of hell for them, but the memorial at the Jacomini's Round Top farm was inspiring and full of grace, an event that encouraged all 300 who attended.

The young family had perished on August 15, 2008, when their rented Cessna crashed into a mountainside southwest of Denver. Their ashes were buried under a glorious old oak tree on the Jacomini farm, in wonderful boxes Tommy Sr. had built himself. Now they were remembered—with the eloquent and meaningful prayers of the priest, with poems, with beautiful violin pieces, and with the release of four white doves, each rising in a different direction, then coming together and flying as a unit until they disappeared into the Texas sky.

Young Tom had earned his pilot's license at fourteen, and three of his best aviator pals saluted him and his family with a flyover in the missing man formation, scraping the treetops. Tears flowed, but so did grace abound. Lunch was a glorious feast, then we all went our separate ways—so aware that life is very hard, but that it is also exquisitely wonderful. Even in the deepest pain and death there is the saving grace of faith, hope, and love.

Within a few days I felt strong enough to fly with Klinka to her house in Park City, Utah. Survivor friends had encouraged me to take a trip. It will raise your spirits, they said, and they were right. My ten days in the Wasatch mountains were blissful. We had lazy days with much fresh food from the farmers' market and lots of good movies, manicures, pedicures, and time on the practice tee. I even had my eyebrows tattooed so I wouldn't have to paint them on after they fell out. The cool weather—mid-70s during the day, in the 40s at night—was a glorious change from the blazing heat of Houston. I flew home a few days before Jim's return from Africa, spoiled rotten, but with a fresh mindset, ready for what lay ahead. I was even okay with all of the hair that was falling out.

Several days before my first chemo treatment I had had my waist-long hair cut off. Deciding I would have fun with this indignity probably helped me to like my short hairdo. "You look twenty-five years younger!" Jim said, almost gleefully, and that certainly helped too! My short do held up well in Utah, but by the time I returned to Houston it was really falling out. Having it all come out in clumps would be discouraging, my friends advised, so I went right to the beauty shop and had it shaved off.

I was prepared because I had gone shopping for wigs early on. Finding a good one was a hard assignment, but fortunately a sweet friend drove me to the wig shop and gave me the moral support I needed as I "tried on the hair." I almost cried over the first ten pieces—they all looked so fake—but after an hour I found one that really worked. I would have left in a puddle of tears if my friend hadn't been there to bring new offerings, cajole me into trying just one more, and encourage me as my spirits flagged. I can't imagine going through something like this without friends like her!

My postoperative period has been very reinforcing. The tender care of my family and friends has made this hard road chockfull of joyful surprises. It's been a time of learning to accept the limitations of illness and age without regret, and to celebrate and appreciate more vigorously the gift of good days and the daily blessings that are too often taken for granted. It's also been a time of learning about many things medical and, especially, of things concerned with diet.

Jim and I thought we were healthy eaters, and we were to a point. Our diets were balanced and nutritious, but our daughters had nudged us for years to go organic, cut down on processed foods, and add more fresh fruits and vegetables. My summer surprise inspired me to read a book that convinced me that our girls were right.

Anticancer: A New Way of Life, a book by David Servan-Schreiber, isn't just another self-help book. The author is a physician, scientist, medical school professor, and cancer survivor. Surgery, chemotherapy, and other convention-al treatments are still the only scientifically proven way to eliminate cancer, he says. But lifestyle changes can help prevent the disease or enhance the benefits of conventional treatment. He writes about a 2005 study by Dr. Dean Ornish in which lifestyle changes by prostate cancer patients clearly arrested the de-velopment of their tumors.

Dr. Servan-Schreiber recommends four approaches. The first is environ-mental; we should avoid pesticides and insecticides, chemical cleaning prod-ucts, and other carcinogenic chemicals, and he says we should also air out dry-cleaned clothes. The second is dietary. He calls the usual American diet "a fertilizer for cancer," and recommends that we cut down on refined sugars, bleached flour, and vegetable oils. Our bodies are designed to process fruit and vegetables, plant-based foods (whole grains, nuts, legumes), fish, and or-ganic meat and eggs. (Patients in the Ornish study followed a strict vegetarian diet with supplements of vitamins, selenium, and omega-3 fatty acids)

The doctor's third recommendation has three parts. He suggests that we engage in more physical activity, that we practice relaxation and meditation exercises, and that we work on accepting our emotions and sharing them hon-estly with others. Finally, Dr. Servan-Schreiber asserts, if we adopt these holistic lifestyle changes, our immune systems will be strengthened and inflammation (a major factor in aging and disease) will be significantly reduced.

It is essential that we become more conscious of the ways that we allow our well-being to be compromised. We are so often conditioned to put work and achievement ahead of everything else, that our health and time spent with those we love suffer as a result. A simple example of this is the common practice of quickly wolfing down a fast-food lunch at our desk instead of taking a little extra time to share a healthier meal and conversation with a friend or coworker. Despite the fact that my office is at home, I have many times been so immersed in my work that I've skipped lunch altogether. Looking back over the past year, I realize that I've rarely even made time to share lunch with a friend. No matter how pressing our work is, our health and our relationships must be respected, valued, and nurtured. These are quality-of-life issues that, taken all together, have a huge impact on our lives.

The message of *Anticancer* really resonates with me. It has helped me understand why cancer and obesity are epidemic in America. Besides all the new chemicals and pollutants that were introduced into the environment after World War II, there were major changes in how animals for market were fed. Instead of having free-range diets, livestock, swine, and poultry were fattened on corn and soybeans; hormones and antibiotics were also introduced and used more heavily. Meat and milk from these animals are suffused with fats and chemicals associated with a higher risk of cancer. Our fast-paced lifestyles —spurred on by the explosion of computers, cell phones, and other technology—have also increased our susceptibility by increasing our stress level. It's a complex issue, and this very light summary certainly doesn't do justice to Dr. Servan-Schreiber's work. Simply put, I strongly recommend the book.

There are many other good books available, and one of my favorites is *The Cancer-Fighting Kitchen* by Rebecca Katz. This book is very informative, and has added some excitement to our meals. The author is a nutrition expert and executive chef who has developed recipes with the minerals, proteins, carbohydrates, phytochemicals, and other nutrients needed by cancer patients. Every ingredient is based on scientific research, and the meals are delicious.

One in every three or four Americans will be diagnosed with cancer. A healthy lifestyle is not a cure-all, but I very much believe it will improve the odds of avoiding the disease or—if you get it anyway—of surviving. It could be so helpful to cancer patients if, upon diagnosis, doctors would provide information about diet and lifestyle changes that could be beneficial in the treatment of the disease. Encouraging patients to take charge of their health is empowering, a good antidote for the sense of helplessness that so many feel when they're told they have cancer.

* * *

There you have it, my summer surprise.

No one can be fully prepared for the mental, emotional, and physical impact of cancer. It's a blow, it hurts, and there's no avoiding that. But the experience is also life-affirming in many ways. Cancer forces you to fight for your life, and in that fight your senses sharpen and your appreciation grows for the many blessings of life: for father and mother, for spouse, sisters, brothers, children, grandchildren and friends. For each day that has gone before and for every new day. The disease challenges you to reexamine your priorities and figure out what really matters in the long run. Too often, too much time is spent on the nonessentials, while important relationships and dreams are shortchanged. Having cancer has made me realize how much our daily choices matter.

A life-threatening disease like cancer puts us face-to-face with our mortality. My relationship with God has deepened during this struggle. An intimate relationship with God is available to us all if we are willing to be honest about who we are with all of our faults, and to accept His gift of unconditional love. Faith means nurturing that honest, loving relationship through good times and bad. Faith can erase fear, even in the valley of the shadow of death. Faith can embolden us to do all things through Him who strengthens us, and to understand that in all things we are more than conquerors through Him who loves us. Faith also teaches that while we, like grass, will wither and die, life in the presence of God is forever bright, shining, and eternal.

ABOUT THE AUTHOR

A ranch girl and a good Catholic, Susan Garrett had married the handsome son of a prominent Houston family. Her life appeared to be on course for happily ever after. When her marriage failed dramatically, it broke her, emotionally and spiritually. Her subsequent marriage to the recently widowed James A. Baker, III, brought their newly blended family—three of hers, four of his, one of theirs into the political sphere of Gerald Ford, Ronald Reagan and George H.W. Bush and led Susan across Texas, to Washington D.C. and around the globe. Her life was fraught with the loneliness and special challenges of being the "wife of" a man engaged in national politics and public service. She struggled with her faith and had a stormy relationship with God.

But, in spite of the stresses she faced with her husband's rising political career, Susan began to put her life back together—by studying the Scriptures, turning things over to God, and praying—for herself, her family and her friends, but also for her adversaries. Once she focused on this reality, she could reach out to others through the Parent's Music Resource Center and the First Lady's Prayer Group, as well as to people of all faiths in a Gathering of Friends held in Jordan and Israel. She learned many of her life lessons the hard way. Now she passes them along—to her children, grandchildren, and others who find this book—with her prayer that readers might learn from her mistakes, find encouragement in her spiritual path, and share a few of the heartfelt moments from her journey.

The text in *Passing It On: An Autobiography with Spirit* is set in Minion, a 1990 Adobe Originals typeface by Robert Slimbach.

Inspired by classical, old style typefaces of the late Renaissance, Minion is an elegant, highly readable type. It combines the aesthetic and functional qualities that make text type highly readable with the versatility of digital technology. Its many ligatures, small caps, oldstyle figures, swashes and other added glyphs provide the designer with unprecedented flexibility and typographic control and lend it beautifully to lengthy text. Minion supports a full range of Western languages, including Greek and Cyrillic. It exhibits a warmth and balance most suitable for the presentation of Susan Baker's story.